am i am i am i am i am i am i am i am i
i am i am i am i am i am i am i am i am i am i am i am i am i am
am i am i am i am i
am i am i am

i am i am i am

        i am i am

Hamlet. Act 1, Scene III

This
above
all
to
thine
own
self
be
true

One of the lasting, endearing images I have of my
dad occurred on one of those short, dull November days.
He'd hide behind our living room door and remained
there until I'd entered the room. As the door slowly
closed behind me, it revealed him pinned up against
the wall with a manic grin on his face, his eyes
rolled back so only the whites seemed to show. It had
the desired effect. I suppose this contributed to
my slightly nervous disposition.

Another memory was when he would grab anything that
resembled a microphone and do a Sinatra impersonation.
This would occur anywhere.

The book is dedicated to my dad

Dear Mr Grain[ger]

1) hesitate to refuse

2) You may include
of the labels,

3) Do not edit, m

4) What an ast
initial encou
had,

Yours f

Wor

...r, 'Do not
...is,
...all' or some

remarks.
...ishing
ter WE (Σ)

...y
Cutler

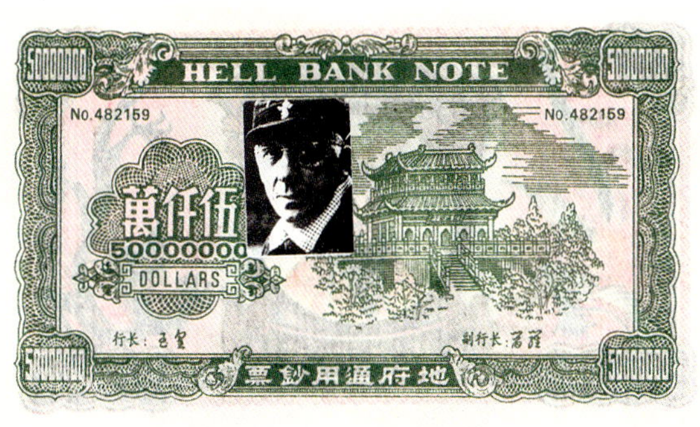

25-3-99 274

When my kid brother
was born, I was three,
& lost my place as
centre of the universe.
I have spent my life
attention-getting.
This is an extremely
common phenomenon, 275
as my experience with
7 to 11 children over
30 years revealed.
I think that the people
in this book have found
their own way of
dealing with the pro-
blem. Of course their
interests are   276
genuine, & they
are guided unconscious-
ly to do what they do, &
are the happier for it.
They have my empathy.
          Ivor Cutler.
          © March 1999

There
was
a
commercial
a
year
or
two
ago.
It showed a man in a suit going off to work.
On the subway he catches the eye of one of the other passengers, a young woman, and pulls
a funny face. It's not a threatening face, or a freaky face, just a friendly funny face.
Immediately the young woman looks away, burying herself back in her newspaper.
There are a number of other vignettes.
In one he passes one of those shop windows full of TVs which film you
as you pass, and he performs a little pirouette.
In another, he halts the bustling flow of pedestrians on a crowded pavement to watch a pigeon wheeling
and soaring in the sky above.
Finally
he ends up in the park. A child there is playing with
a model sailing boat on the pond.
But the boat has gone out of reach and he can't get it back, so he's just standing on the shore,
watching it impotently and looking woebegone.
Our hero sees the problem and, without so much as rolling up the trousers of his suit, wades into the
pond to fetch it. He reunites the boat with its overjoyed owner.
As he does so the child's mother hurries up, pulls the child away from him and
scolds him for speaking to strangers.
At this point we fade to black and some words come up on the screen:
'Is he mad? Or is everyone else?'

antony woodward

In winter one just exists. For the rest of the year there is camp and clothing maintenance and modifications, canoeing, walking, just looking and watching, and all the normal household jobs – but everything takes far longer to complete. My nearest neighbours are across 2km of water and I have a choice of 2 canoes for transport. To walk out means covering 2½ miles of deer track bog and forestry paths; and I am bone idle.

I like reading: naval historical fiction, Southern African history, Ayn Rand's two main novels – many times each – and religion. I like listening to Beethoven and Sibelius, ballet, Gilbert and Sullivan, Gregorian chant and the Drums and Pipes. I am never bored and am only lonely when in a crowd.

Aided by a little winkle picking and a part time job on a nearby fish farm for a while I managed quite well after I took myself off social welfare in March 1989. Since then the tattoo has only supported me, without aid from anything else, for a year and, apart from the paradise in which I live the bottom has dropped out of my life. But that is another story. Even in Paradise the devil rears his ugly head, but then, that's where he started off too.

Tom Leppard

LOCH NA BEISTE
ISLE OF SKYE

20 April 1997.

tom leppard

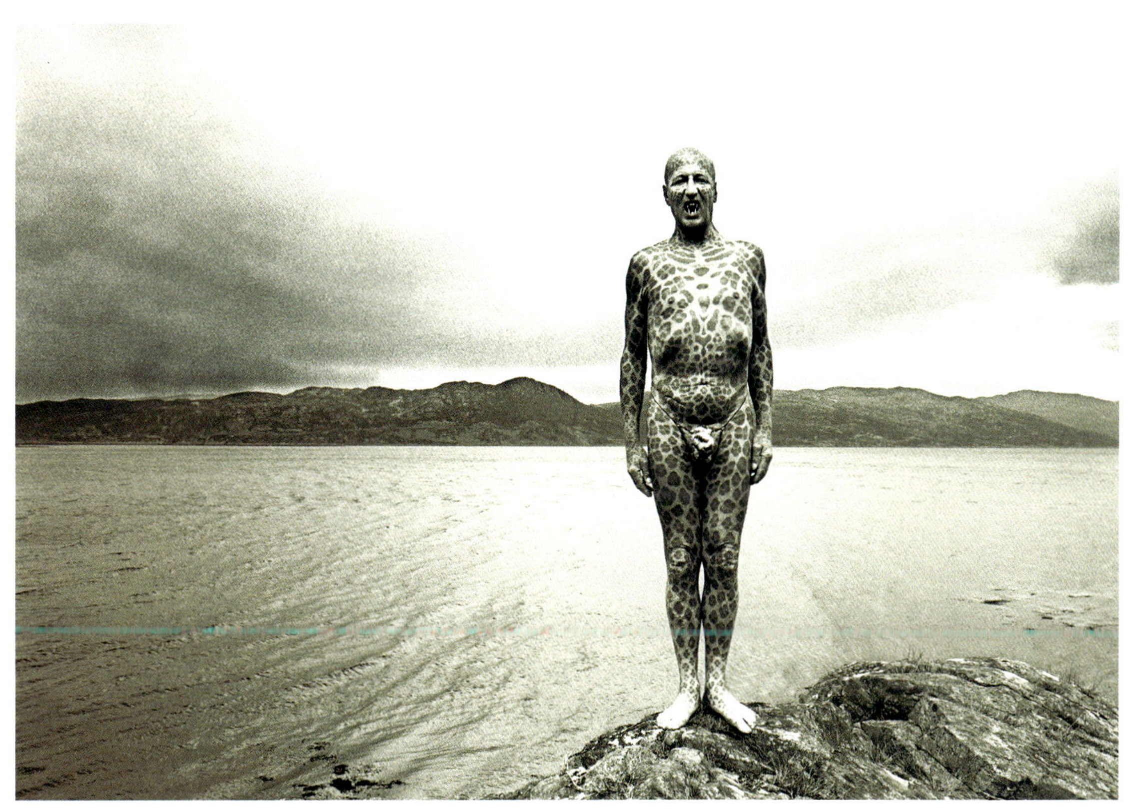

My name is Arthur, I am he,
Once and future, born to be,

Celtic Chieftain, Knight of old,
I am the story as was fortold.

Loyal Knights, must come to me,
bowing to their destiny.

Each of them a worthy Knight,
Standing for what's Just and right.

A Code of Chivalry, follow we most,
to speak the truth, be honourable and Just.

Where'ere we find them, we'll right wrong,
for this must always be our song.

The Couldron and the Cross unite,
Christian and Pagan, join our fight.

re-Unite Our Celtic Creed,
in its time of Greatest need.

Celtic Minstrels, rise and sing,
Now is the time, of the future King.

The time is now, we wait no more,
for Arthur's back, and will restore.

Arrived on Avalon, Eighty Seven,
Arthur Pendragon, June Eleven. © '87

KING ARTHUR PENDRAGON.
Honoured Pendragon, Glastonbury Order of Druids.
Official Swordbearer, Secular Order of Druids.
Titular head & Choosen Chief, Loyal Arthurian Warband.
a member of the Council of British Druid Orders.
Bard of the free Gorsedd of Caer Abiri.
Swordbearer to the Cotswold Order of Druids.
Champion of the free & Open Gorsedd of Caer Badan.
Member of the Ancient and Modern Order of Druids.
Honourary member of the Berengaria & South downs Dragon Orders.

Arthur Roc '97 /I\

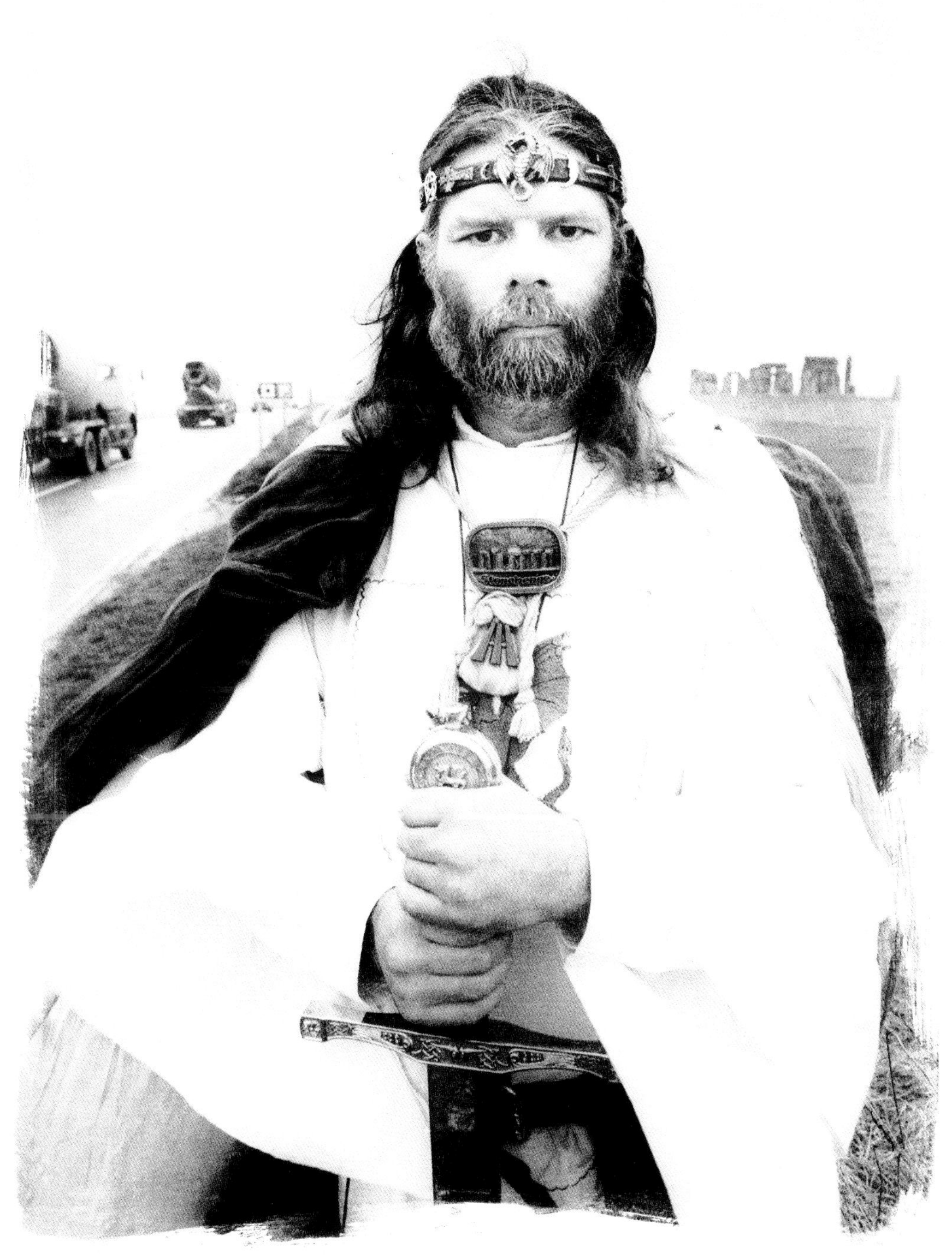

king arthur

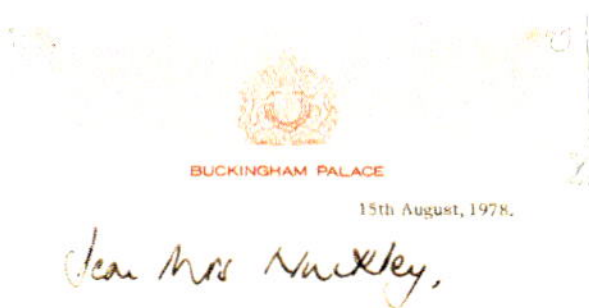

BUCKINGHAM PALACE

15th August, 1978.

Dear Mrs Nuckley,

Princess Anne has asked me to write and thank you for your birthday greetings.

Her Royal Highness was most touched that you had remembered the occasion of her birthday and thought of her in this way.

The Princess sends her warmest thanks.

Yours sincerely,

Lady in Waiting to
HRH The Princess Anne,
Mrs Mark Phillips.

Mrs M. Nuckley.

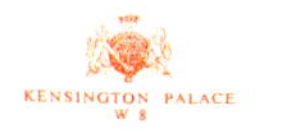

KENSINGTON PALACE
W 8

22nd August, 1978

Dear Mrs. Nuckley,

I am bidden by Princess Margaret to write and thank you very sincerely for your splendid card and the enclosed verse.

Her Royal Highness greatly appreciated your kind message of good wishes.

Yours sincerely,

Lady-in-Waiting

Mrs. May Nuckley.

BUCKINGHAM PALACE

From M.M. Colborne, Esq.

1st December, 1978

Dear Mrs Nuckley,

The Prince of Wales has instructed me to thank you for your card and present sent for his 30th birthday.

His Royal Highness was most pleased to receive your magnificent card and the cassette, which will be most useful, and thanks you sincerely for remembering his birthday in this fashion.

I am returning your photograph as I feel sure you would wish to keep it.

Yours sincerely,

for Secretary

Mrs. M. Nuckley.

WINDSOR CASTLE

21st April, 19..

Dear Mrs Nuckley,

I am commanded by The Queen to write and thank you for the beautifully executed card and the pen which you have sent to Her Majesty with your good wishes on the occasion of her birthday.

The Queen was most touched to see your verse, and Her Majesty thought it was very kind of you to make this lovely card for her.

The Queen much appreciated your thought for her at this time, and I am to send to you Her Majesty's most sincere thanks.

Yours sincerely,

Lady-in-Waiting

Mrs. Nuckley,
19, Lower Grade Road,
St. Leonards,
Sussex.

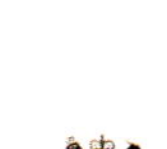

10 DOWNING STREET

17 May 1979

Dear Mrs. Nuckley,

The Prime Minister has asked me to thank you for the splendid card which you sent her.

Mrs. Thatcher is grateful to you for your congratulations and good wishes.

Yours sincerely,

Mrs. Nuckley.

Owing to the fact that over 30,000 letters and cards were received on the occasion of Her Majesty's 80th birthday, we regret the delay in thanking you.

LADY-IN-WAITING

28-3-98

I am May Fisher, I have always been Royalist. So when my children grew up I decided I'd do something unusual with my life. In 1978 I made Birthday cards for some of the Royal Family. The Queen Mother, The Queen, Princess Anne, Princess Margaret. Later when Prince Charles was engaged to (Princess Di) Lady Diana Spencer I made them an engagement card, & I was delighted when I got a letter from Lady Diana Spencer herself thanking me for my Homemade card & so actually signed in her own handwriting. Also I made a Wedding card for them both in 1981 & received a 'Thankyou' letter from them. I made a 3 piece outfit to celebrate their Wedding, all made out of souvenir Tea-Towels with their faces imprinted into the material & dressed up a Sunhat to match. I was so proud that I paraded all along our Town & Seafront in it. & on their Anniversary each year till they split up. Then in 1983 I myself was married & I wore that very outfit just to be different. I was so proud of it too & I just loved Princess Di. I made her Birthday cards every year right up to 1997. & she always wrote to thank me. I'm still devastated about her untimely death along with Dodi Fayed just when she had found happiness. How cruel. I've been mentioned in the 'Alternative Book of Records"

2

for my outfit as "the worlds only Wedding Dress made from Charles & Diana Commemorative Tea Towels made by me in 1983" & was also shown on T.V. for several years later as I was interviewed for Meridian News. I have had another outfit made in 1980 of Union Jack Tea-Towels which are worn every year to celebrate The Queen & Queen Mothers Birthday, & also when Princess Margaret & Princess Anne came to our Town, & when the Queen came here to open our New Shopping Centre in 1997.

Another unusual Hobby of mine is collecting Wrigleys chewing-gum labels since 1984, all of the strips of gum I have chewed my way through, which is 7,500 so far.

Another Hobby is collecting film, Radio & T.V. stars signed Photos I have about 200 including Ronald Reagan & his wife, & our New Prime Minister Tony Blair, & some of the Royals Family. Chewing gum labels are mentioned in the Alternative Book of Records too. I make Valentine cards all unique my own Designs & Xmas & Birthday cards for Family & friends, & T.V. presenters, I've been mentioned as the Bee Gee's oldest Fan & Elton Johns too.   May Fisher

---

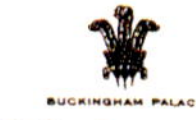

BUCKINGHAM PALACE

From: The Lady Diana Spencer   15th May, 1981

Dear Mrs Nuckley,

The Prince of Wales joins me in thanking you for sending us such a charming card. You have made it most beautifully and have obviously spent a great amount of time and trouble collecting and pressing all the flowers.

His Royal Highness and I are deeply touched by your kind thought and once again we thank you most sincerely.

Yours sincerely,

Diana Spencer.

Mrs. May Nuckley

BUCKINGHAM PALACE

From Miss A. Beckwith-Smith

26 November 1981

The Princess of Wales has asked me to thank you for your kind letter and message of congratulations and good wishes.

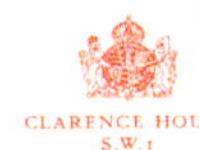

CLARENCE HOUSE
S.W.1

Dear Mrs Nuckley,

Queen Elizabeth The Queen Mother bids me thank you for your message of birthday greetings.

The Queen Mother wishes me to tell you that her birthday this year was a particularly happy one, with the joy of the wedding of The Prince and Princess of Wales and Her Majesty's own return to health.

Yours sincerely,

Lady-in-Waiting

BUCKINGHAM PALACE

From Miss A. Beckwith-Smith

22 December 1981

BRITISH BROADCASTING CORPORATION
LIME GROVE STUDIOS, LONDON W12 7RJ
TELEPHONE 01 743 8000 TELEX 265781
TELEGRAMS AND CABLES: TELECASTS LONDON TELEX

Personal & Private

27th October 1981

Dear Mrs Nuckley,

How very kind of you to take the trouble to send me such a splendid birthday card. I was very touched by the message it contained.

With many thanks and best wishes.

Yours sincerely

Sir Robin Day

Mrs. May Nuckley,
19 Glassfield Road,
St. Leonards-on-Sea,
East Sussex.

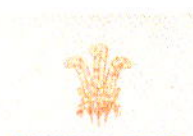

BUCKINGHAM PALACE

17th November, 1981

Dear Mrs Nuckley,

The Prince and Princess of Wales have asked me to write and thank you for your very kind thought in writing to them on the occasion of their marriage.

Their Royal Highnesses were most touched by the good wishes you have expressed and have asked me to send you their very sincere thanks.

Yours sincerely,

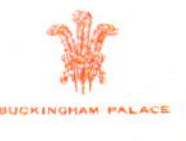

BUCKINGHAM PALACE

From: Miss A. Beckwith-Smith   19th July, 1982

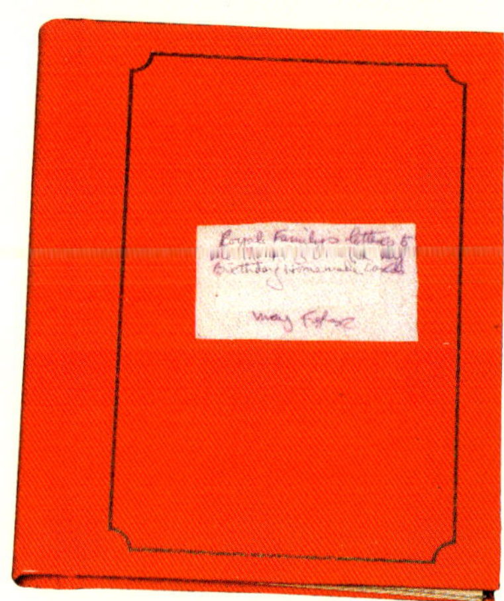

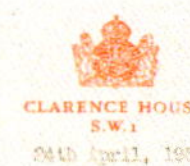

CLARENCE HOUSE
S.W.1
24th April, 1953

Dear Mrs. Nuckley,

Queen Elizabeth The Queen Mother has asked me to write to you and thank you very much for the congratulations you sent to Her Majesty.

The loyal sentiments you expressed so clearly on your wedding day are appreciated by The Queen Mother, who bids me convey to you and your husband her best wishes for the future.

Yours sincerely,

Elizabeth Basset.
Lady-in-Waiting.

Mrs. T. Nuckley.

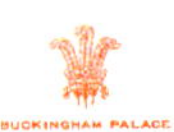

BUCKINGHAM PALACE

From The Hon. Mrs. Vivian Baring

6 July 1983

Dear Mrs Nuckley,

The Princess of Wales has asked me to send you her thanks for your special card of good wishes to Prince William on his first birthday.

Her Royal Highness is most grateful to you for taking the trouble to make the three horses for her son.

The Princess sends you her thanks and best wishes.

Yours sincerely,

Lavinia Baring
Lady-in-Waiting

Mrs. Nuckley.

BUCKINGHAM PALACE

22nd July, 1983

Dear Mrs Nuckley,

thank you very much for your card.

Her Royal Highness was most grateful for your good wishes and has asked me to send you her very sincere thanks.

Yours sincerely,

Anne Beckwith-Smith
Lady-in-Waiting

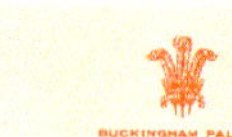

CLARENCE HOUSE
S.W.1
2nd August, 1983

Dear Mrs. Nuckley,

Queen Elizabeth The Queen Mother was greatly touched to receive your good wishes on the occasion of her birthday and I am to thank you most warmly for your kind message of greetings to Her Majesty.

I am also returning the photograph you sent, as The Queen Mother feels sure that it is precious to you.

Yours sincerely,

Ruth Fermoy
Lady-in-Waiting

Mrs. Nuckley.

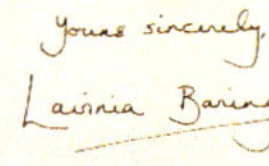

BUCKINGHAM PALACE

From The Hon. Mrs. Vivian Baring

2nd March, 1984

Dear Mrs. Nuckley,

The Prince and Princess of Wales have asked me to pass on their warmest thanks for your kind message of good wishes.

Their Royal Highnesses were most touched by your kind thought in sending the delightful hand made card.

Thank you again for writing and The Prince and Princess ask me to send you their sincere thanks and best wishes.

Yours sincerely,

Lavinia Baring
Lady-in-Waiting

Mrs. Nuckley

BUCKINGHAM PALACE

From Lady-in-Waiting to H.R.H. The Princess of Wales

26th June 1984

Dear Mrs Nuckley,

The Princess of Wales has asked me to thank you so much for the lovely card you sent on the occasion of Prince William's second birthday.

Her Royal Highness was most touched by your kind thought in sending this delightful card and asks me to send you her sincere thanks and best wishes.

Yours sincerely,

Anne Beckwith-Smith
Miss A. Beckwith-Smith

Mrs May Nuckley.

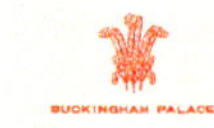

BUCKINGHAM PALACE

From Lady-in-Waiting to H.R.H. The Princess of Wales

9th July 1984

Dear Mrs Nuckley,

The Princess of Wales has asked me to thank you so much for the lovely card you sent on the occasion of Prince William's second birthday.

Her Royal Highness was most touched by your kind thought in sending this delightful card and asks me to send you her sincere thanks and best wishes.

Yours sincerely,

Anne Beckwith-Smith
Miss A. Beckwith-Smith

BUCKINGHAM PALACE

From The Assistant Private Secretary to H.R.H. The Prince of Wales

22nd November, 1984.

Dear Mrs Nuckley,

The Prince of Wales has asked me to thank you for your kind message of congratulations sent on the occasion of his birthday.

His Royal Highness is grateful to you for taking the trouble to write as you did and has asked me to send you his warmest thanks and best wishes.

Yours Sincerely,

David Roycroft.

Mrs. Mary Nuckley.

BUCKINGHAM PALACE

From Lady-in-Waiting to H.R.H. The Princess of Wales

28th June, 1985

Dear Mrs. Nuckley

The Princess of Wales has asked me to thank you very much for your message of good wishes which you kindly sent on the occasion of Prince William's third birthday.

Her Royal Highness was most touched by your kind thought and has asked me to send you her sincere thanks and best wishes.

Yours sincerely

Hazel West
Mrs. George West.

BUCKINGHAM PALACE

From Lady-in-Waiting to H.R.H. The Princess of Wales

12th July, 1985

Dear Mrs. Nuckley

The Princess of Wales has asked me to thank you very much for your message of good wishes which you kindly sent on the occasion of her birthday.

Her Royal Highness was most touched by your kind thought and has asked me to send you her sincere thanks and best wishes.

Yours sincerely

Hazel West
Mrs. George West.

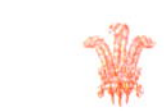

BUCKINGHAM PALACE

From Lady-in-Waiting to H.R.H. The Princess of Wales

7th August, 1985

Dear Mrs. Nuckley

The Prince and Princess of Wales have asked me to thank you very much for your message of good wishes which you kindly sent on the occasion of Their Royal Highnesses' Wedding Anniversary.

The Prince and Princess of Wales were most touched by your kind thought and have asked me to send you their sincere thanks and best wishes.

Yours sincerely,

Sarah Campden
Viscountess Campden

BUCKINGHAM PALACE

14th August, 1985

Dear Mrs Nuckley

Princess Anne has asked me to write and thank you for your beautiful birthday card which she was most touched to receive.

I have been asked to sent you The Princess's very best wishes.

Lieutenant Colonel Peter Gibbs
Private Secretary to
H.R.H. The Princess Anne, Mrs Mark Phillips

Mrs. Mary Nuckley

KENSINGTON PALACE
W.8

22nd August, 1985

Dear Mrs. Nuckley,

Princess Margaret bids me send you her sincere thanks for your message of good wishes on the occasion of her birthday.

I am to tell you that Her Royal Highness greatly appreciated your kind greetings.

Yours sincerely,

Lady-in-Waiting

Mrs. May Nuckley.

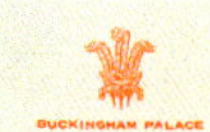

BUCKINGHAM PALACE

From Lady-in-Waiting to H.R.H. The Princess of Wales

24th September, 1985.

Dear Mrs Nuckley,

The Princess of Wales has asked me to thank you very much for your message of good wishes which you kindly sent on the occasion of Prince Henry's first birthday.

Her Royal Highness was most touched by your kind thought and has asked me to send you her sincere thanks and best wishes.

Yours sincerely,

Anne Beckwith-Smith
Miss A. Beckwith-Smith.

From: Major The Hon Andrew Wigram

BUCKINGHAM PALACE

11th June 1986

Dear Mrs Nuckley,

The Duke of Edinburgh has asked me to thank you for your good wishes on his birthday.

His Royal Highness was very grateful to you for your kind thought.

Yours Sincerely,

Andrew Wigram

Mrs May Nuckley

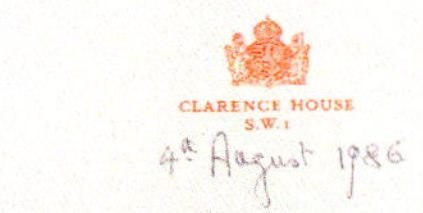

CLARENCE HOUSE
S.W.1

4th August 1986

Dear Mrs Nuckley,

Queen Elizabeth The Queen Mother has asked me to write and thank you very much indeed for your kind thought of Her Majesty on the …

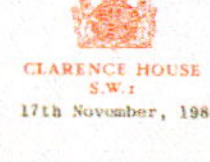

CLARENCE HOUSE
S.W.1

17th November, 1986

Dear Mrs. Nuckley,

I am bidden by Queen Elizabeth The Queen Mother to thank you for your card, and for your kind thought of her at this time.

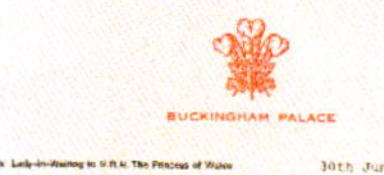

BUCKINGHAM PALACE

From Lady-in-Waiting to H.R.H. The Princess of Wales

30th June 1987

Dear Mrs. Nuckley,

The Princess of Wales has asked me to thank you for your kind message of good wishes which you sent to Prince William on the occasion of his fifth birthday.

Her Royal Highness was most grateful …

BUCKINGHAM PALACE

29th April 1988

Dear Mrs Nuckley,

I write to thank you very much for the kind message of good wishes you have sent The Queen for her birthday.

Her Majesty is at present in Australia but I know she would wish me to thank you most sincerely for your message, which she will receive on her return to this country.

Yours sincerely,
J. Chamberlain
Lady-in-Waiting

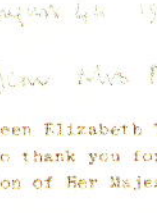

CLARENCE HOUSE
S.W.1

August 4th 1988

Dear Mrs Nuckley

Queen Elizabeth The Queen Mother has asked me to thank you for remembering her on the occasion of Her Majesty's 88th birthday.

The Queen Mother greatly appreciated your thought for her at this time.

Yours sincerely,
Frances Campbell Preston
Lady-in-Waiting

Mrs M. Nuckley

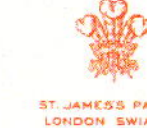

ST. JAMES'S PALACE
LONDON SWIA IBS

From: The Assistant Private Secretary and Lady-in-Waiting to H.R.H. The Princess of Wales

23rd June 1989

Dear Mrs Nuckley,

The Princess of Wales has asked me to thank you very much for your kind message of good wishes which you sent to Prince William on the occasion of his seventh birthday.

Her Royal Highness was most touched by your kind thought and has asked me to send you her warmest thanks and best wishes.

Yours sincerely,
Anne Beckwith-Smith

Mrs M. Nuckley   Miss Anne Beckwith-Smith

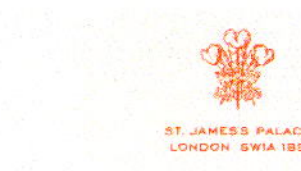

ST. JAMES'S PALACE
LONDON SWIA IBS

From: The Lady-in-Waiting to H.R.H. The Princess of Wales

5th July 1990

Dear Mrs Nuckley,

The Princess of Wales has asked me to thank you so very much for your kind greetings which you sent on the occasion of her birthday.

Her Royal Highness was most touched by your kind thought and has asked me to send you her thanks and best wishes.

Yours sincerely,
Jean Rae.

Mrs Fay Pike

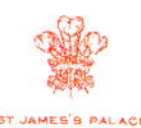

ST. JAMES'S PALACE
LONDON SWIA IBS

N°1

Dear Mrs Fisher,

The Prince and Princess of Wales were very touched by your kind and generous message of good wishes for Prince William and wanted to thank you most warmly for your concern.

Their Royal Highnesses were extremely grateful.

Yours sincerely,
Jean Rae.

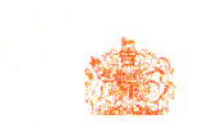

BUCKINGHAM PALACE

April 24 1992

Dear Mrs Fisher,

I write at The Queen's command to thank you for the good wishes you have sent to Her Majesty for her birthday.

Your thought for The Queen at this time is greatly appreciated and I am to thank you so much for your kind message.

Yours sincerely
Esme Cromer
Lady-in-Waiting

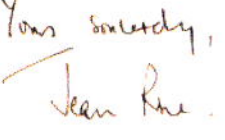

BUCKINGHAM PALACE

3rd May 1993

Dear Mrs Fisher,

I am commanded by The Queen to thank you so much for the message of good wishes you sent Her Majesty for her birthday.

The Queen appreciated your kind thought in remembering her at this time and I am to thank you again for writing as you did.

Yours sincerely
Mary Morrison.
Lady-in-Waiting

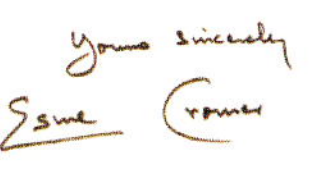

CLARENCE HOUSE
S.W.1

6th August 1993

Dear Mrs Fisher

I am bidden by Queen Elizabeth The Queen Mother to thank you most warmly for the greetings you have sent on the occasion of Her Majesty's birthday.

It has indeed given The Queen Mother much happiness to receive your thoughtful expression of good wishes.

Yours sincerely,
Frances Campbell Preston
Lady-in-Waiting

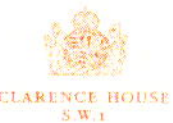

BUCKINGHAM PALACE

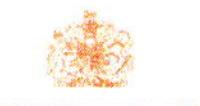

BUCKINGHAM PALACE

21st April 1992

Dear Mrs Fisher,

I am commanded by The Queen to write and thank you so much for sending good wishes to Her Majesty for her birthday, and for the press clipping and photograph, taken of her birthday last year, which you enclosed.

The Queen is touched by your loyalty and affection for her and her family, and thought it was kind of you to send her your happy photograph.

I am sorry it is not possible to send you a photograph owing to Her Majesty's wishes in these matters, but I am to thank you once again for your kind and your good wishes which The Queen much appreciates.

Yours sincerely,
Mary Morrison.
Lady-in-Waiting

Mrs M. Fisher.

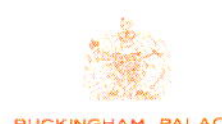

CLARENCE HOUSE
S.W.1

1996

Your kind message to Queen Elizabeth The Queen Mother has been received with much pleasure.

The Queen Mother has asked me to write to thank you for these birthday wishes, and the picture you did especially for Her Majesty, which add so much to the happiness of the occasion.

Yours sincerely,
Margaret Rhodes
Lady-in-Waiting

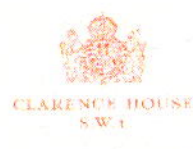

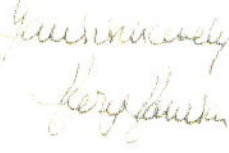

CLARENCE HOUSE
S.W.1

2nd August 1995

Dear Mrs Fisher

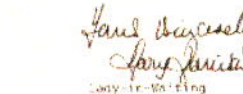

CLARENCE HOUSE
S.W.1

22nd November 1995

Dear Mrs. Fisher,

I have been asked by Queen Elizabeth The Queen Mother to thank you so much for your kind message of good wishes and the photographs

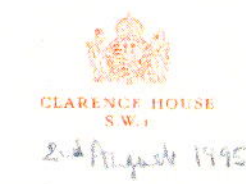

CLARENCE HOUSE
S.W.1

21st August 1996

Dear Mrs Fisher

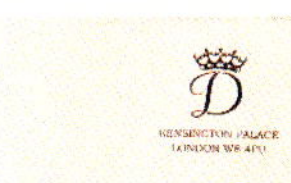

KENSINGTON PALACE
LONDON W8 4PU

From: The Office of The Prince of Wales

28th July 1997

Dear Mrs Fisher,

The Princess of Wales has asked me to thank you for your wonderful card and kind birthday greetings. The Princess was delighted to hear from you and has asked me to send you her best wishes.

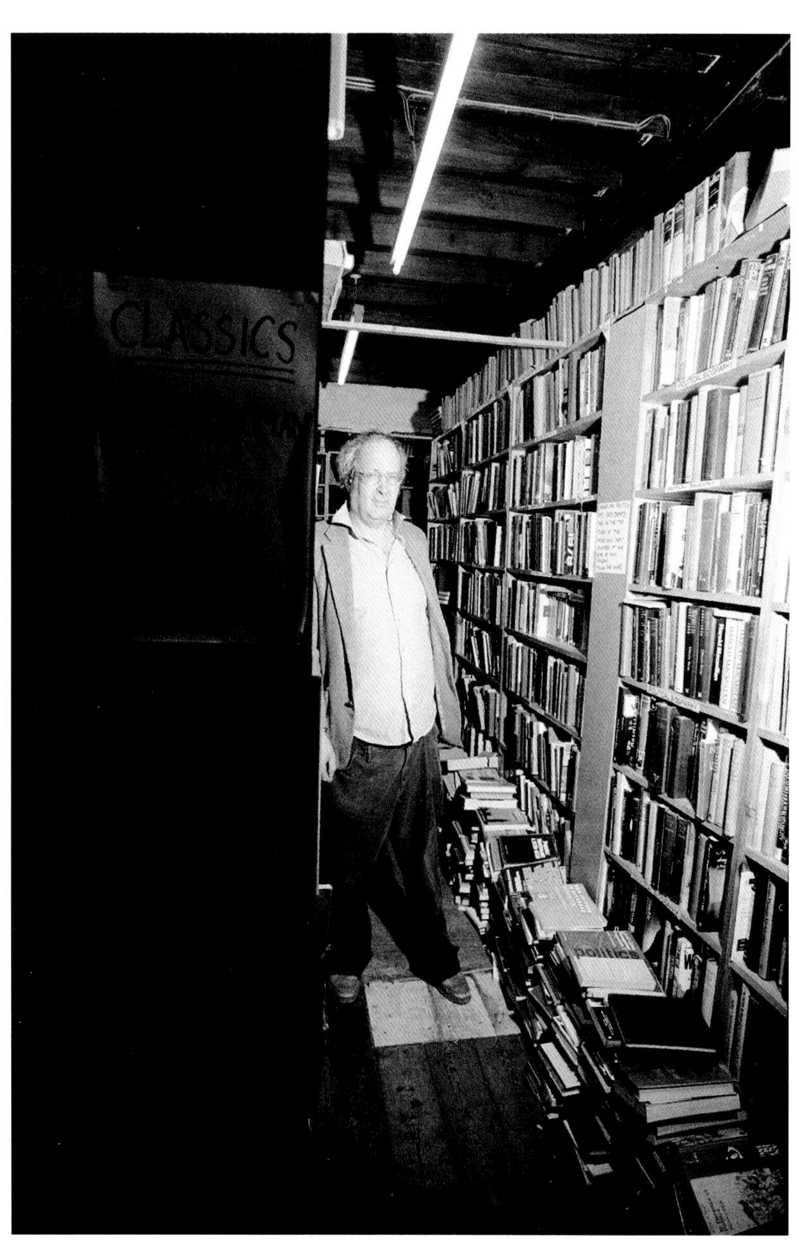

richard
booth

I am Richard Booth. I went West from school
- nearly everybody else went East. I became frightened
of the reality created by the Quangos - Tourist Boards, Development
Boards and perhaps therefore spent the rest of my life
like a butterfly trying to fly through a pane of glass.

Richard Booth

Higham Ferrers,
Northants.

October 28th, circa 1998.... and as I write this, its raining, gales blowing and I understand its even worse outside, but you can't go by mere rumours, of course..

Now, just where do we start on this? - you see, dear reader, the nice man who took my photograph for this book also said that he wanted me to write "something as to why I do what I do....", so to the best of my ability in the written sense, the following is for your benefit and if any of it makes sense, please be sure to let me know in the passing of time.

I am, they tell me, an 'eccentric'. I don't actually agree on that as I take the view that its me that is okay and the rest of you lot are the one's that should be wearing that label. You see, I take the line that I want to live my life MY way, not how 'I should', compared to the rest of the people/ sheep that seem to take Life as being part of some bland, plodding herd that does not seem to have an aim other than propping the local bar up, watching the 'telly' etc. and excitement consisting of one's pen running out of ink just before the Lottery balls are coming out.....

I firmly believe that you should do what YOU want to do, never mind the others around you that tell you otherwise, and then you have an aim, not just doing 'what the others do', after all, its your Life, do what YOU want to do, within your capability, as humans have mastered the art of flying and for the more adventurous among you, it should be pointed out that obtaining monies from financial outlets, i.e. banks, with the aid of a loaded weapon is considered a trifle 'iffy', so its best left to various governments that seem to crop up every now and again to do it with less fuss and palaver, forms are available from your local Post Office for this purpose, but don't ask on a Tuesday as its 'pension day' and the staff are usually quite busy.....

So - there you have it really. I am of the understanding that we have but one 'go' at this crazy game called "Life" and unlike video, no 'replay button', so its up to us all, not just me, to 'get on with it' and do what we want to do, never mind what those across the road think, its what YOU think that really matters, so get going NOWWWWWWW!!!!!

Yours most thingy and all that sort of thing!

John Ward
(Inventist)

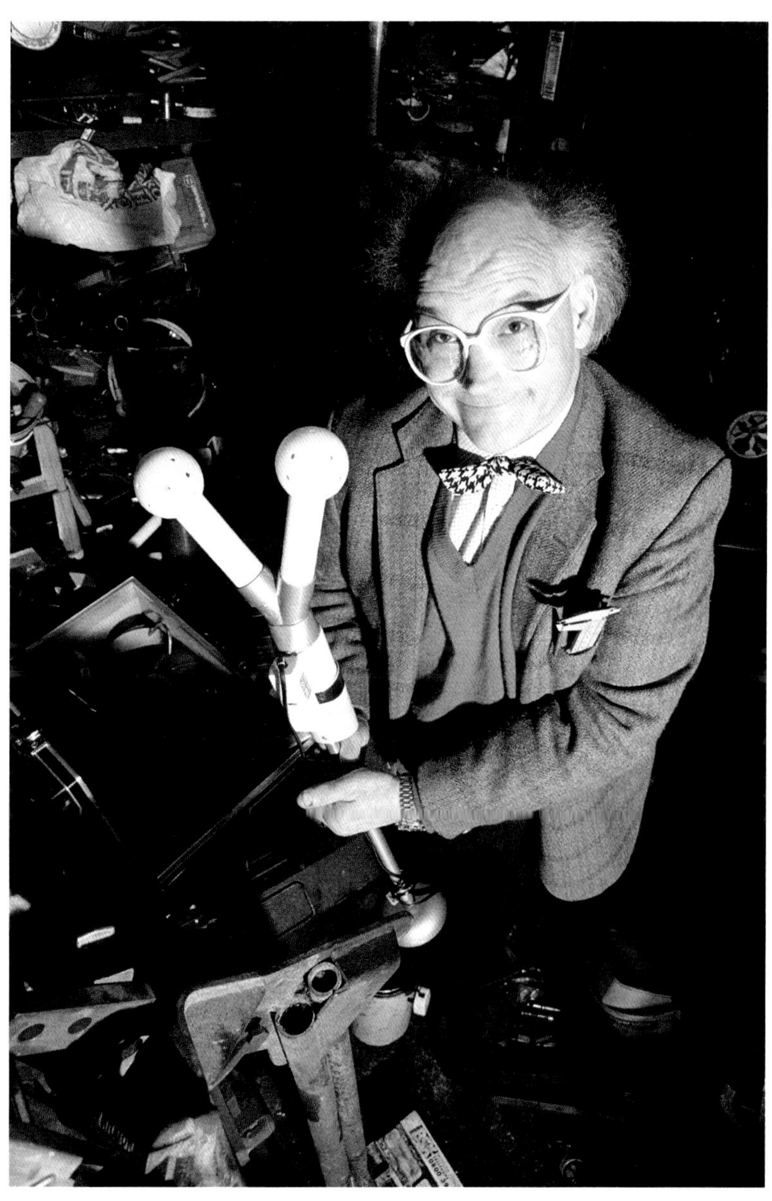

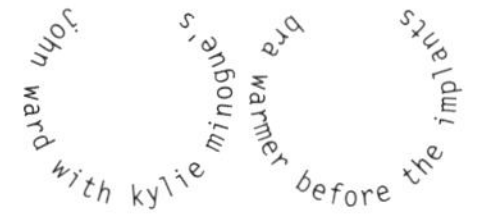

john ward with kylie minogue's bra warmer before the implants

Life of one of the last woodcraftsmen.

I am a Coppice Merchant and work and live in each coppice in Gloucestershire and Wiltshire.
As coppicing is done in a cycle manner, cutting 5 to 10 acres in each coppice. I live a nomadic way of life and work in isolated places, and live in harmony with nature.
Some people say I am unique, as I live a very humble lifestyle and have very few concessions on modern life.
I am also one of the last remaining Luddites – using no machines.
If I need trees cut down I get a woodcutter to do it with his

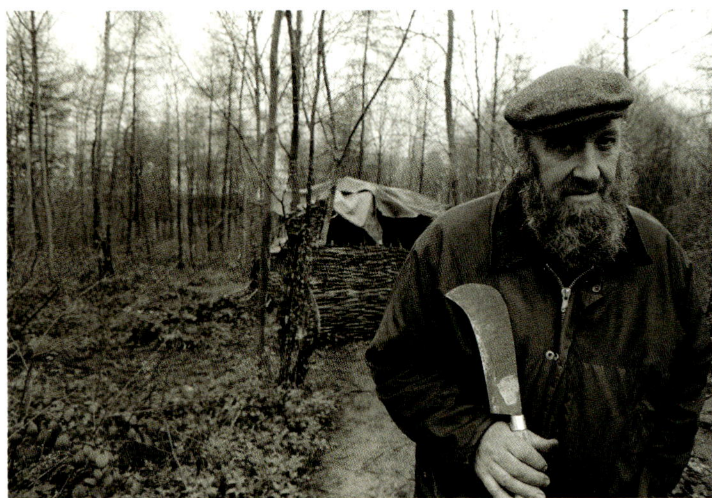

bodger bodger

chainsaw, all I use is hand tools.
I live in a bender or shelter all year and also use a bender as a workshop.
Most of my work is carried out in private woods on one large estate. Therefore very few members of the public see me at work.
This way of life has gone on for thousands of years in the countryside yet I am a Londoner.
I also carry out research and experiments in all aspects of coppice management and the changing attitudes towards the countryside and agriculture.
Having served six years in the army has helped me no end, for to be able to live such a lifestyle one needs self-discipline and must be able to cope with all sorts of situations
I not only have to cut the coppice ones but make many different sorts of coppice products some being traditional example – besoms – wattle hurdles – thatching spron-cleths pegs – pea sticks – bean poles – garden furniture etc I also have to manage the wildlife so it is all in harmony with nature.
This mean deer – squirrel – birds etc and not surgassing the

(3)

the insect: world which is also part of nature which most people do not see. Also all the glora and fauna.
So coppicing is a very diverse way of forest management and of nature conservation
To survive in the outdoors you need shelter – water all general.
and the shops can be many miles away, and even if they were nearby if one was to shop there all the time, it could take a large part of your day up so one also has to manage time as well, for the weather can be against you.
Water is collected from a spring if there is one in a coppice or you have to collect the rain water.
The shelter or bender is made from mostly hazle poles by bending them over and pegging them in the ground with a canvas over them.
You also need fuel. This comes from some of the trees and shrubs you cut for making charcoal.
I use a Bar-B-Q to cook on and in the evening after cooking my dinner and the smoke has gone I then keep it into the bender for heat, after topping it up.

(4)

This can last for 3 to 4 hours with a temperature of up to 70F yet it could be freezing outside and I sitting there with a T-shirt on.
Most people today use a micro wave oven. I use a biscuit tin which does the same job, and is far cheaper. Cake Aroma puts can be used in the same way. if they have a lid.
Newspaper cost you a lot of money each week but I have them given to use to light the fire or get the charcoal burner going. But since I read them to keep me up to what is going on out there and at Congress!
I could have a TV if I wanted but I prefer to do without but have a radio
TV is a con, I find. someone will else is going to make money out of you by way of the adverts especially children.
Most basic good is obtained very cheaply from the countryside and save these journeys into a town or village and carrying it back.
I get meat by way of someone nearby shooting rabbits – deer – squirrel yes even squirrel as today these are sold in restaurants, to make a pie pigon – crow – magpie is nice if you into a grouple

Veg can be got from local peoples
gardens or from the local farmers.
Mushrooms and fungus can be FOUND
IN from the wood
Even alcohol can be found in a
wood. This is made from the sap
of some of the tree's you find in
a coppice.
Fruit and nuts can also be found
and apart from food for
yourself you can also sell
these or in exchange along for
alcohol in your local pub as
well as the mushrooms and fungus.
As I [illegible] of these goods are seasonal
you will have to buy a small amount
of food in the local shops.
My transport is a push bike or
I walk every were.
I enjoy my way of life and that
of isolation and the tranquillity
but also understand a human needs
the company of other humans.
The pub is never far away. and get
old friends as well as new ones come
to see me and stay for 2 or 3 days.
Alas this way of life could come
to a end if the LPA - Local
planning Authority have their way.
After all these thousands of years
of a sustainable lifestyle.
Stroud District council
Gloucestershire.

is claiming that because I [illegible] use
a coppice I have changed the use
of the land that being RESIDENTIAL
and therefore need planning permission
I have therefore appealed against
this and there will be a public
inquiry on the 18-1-98.
The dictionary meaning of RESIDENTIAL
is private houses - RESIDENT mean-
residing - permanent - inhabitant.
I claim, I am None of these.
It would seem to me that
bureaucracy and authority have gone
over the top with these un-needed
laws - regulations and controls.
If I lose this case then many
people in the coppicing industry will
become unemployed and another
or our ancient traditional skills
could be lost.
With 25-000 farmers already gone
out of business who alone had the
skills needed to manage the
countryside.

Could you send me a copy of the
tape you will use.

yours sincerely
Rodger White

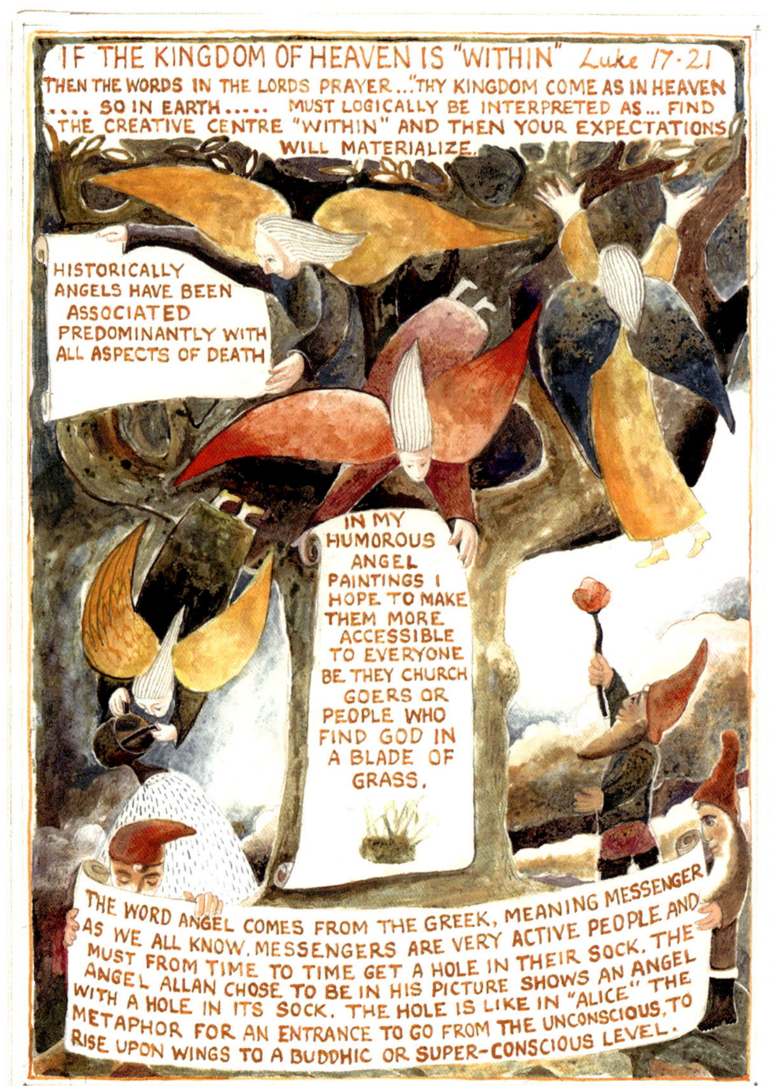

IF THE KINGDOM OF HEAVEN IS "WITHIN" Luke 17·21
THEN THE WORDS IN THE LORDS PRAYER..."THY KINGDOM COME AS IN HEAVEN
.... SO IN EARTH ..... MUST LOGICALLY BE INTERPRETED AS ... FIND
THE CREATIVE CENTRE "WITHIN" AND THEN YOUR EXPECTATIONS
WILL MATERIALIZE.

HISTORICALLY
ANGELS HAVE BEEN
ASSOCIATED
PREDOMINANTLY WITH
ALL ASPECTS OF DEATH

IN MY
HUMOROUS
ANGEL
PAINTINGS I
HOPE TO MAKE
THEM MORE
ACCESSIBLE
TO EVERYONE
BE THEY CHURCH
GOERS OR
PEOPLE WHO
FIND GOD IN
A BLADE OF
GRASS.

THE WORD ANGEL COMES FROM THE GREEK, MEANING MESSENGER
AS WE ALL KNOW. MESSENGERS ARE VERY ACTIVE PEOPLE AND
MUST FROM TIME TO TIME GET A HOLE IN THEIR SOCK. THE
ANGEL ALLAN CHOSE TO BE IN HIS PICTURE SHOWS AN ANGEL
WITH A HOLE IN ITS SOCK. THE HOLE IS LIKE IN "ALICE" THE
METAPHOR FOR AN ENTRANCE TO GO FROM THE UNCONSCIOUS, TO
RISE UPON WINGS TO A BUDDHIC OR SUPER-CONSCIOUS LEVEL.

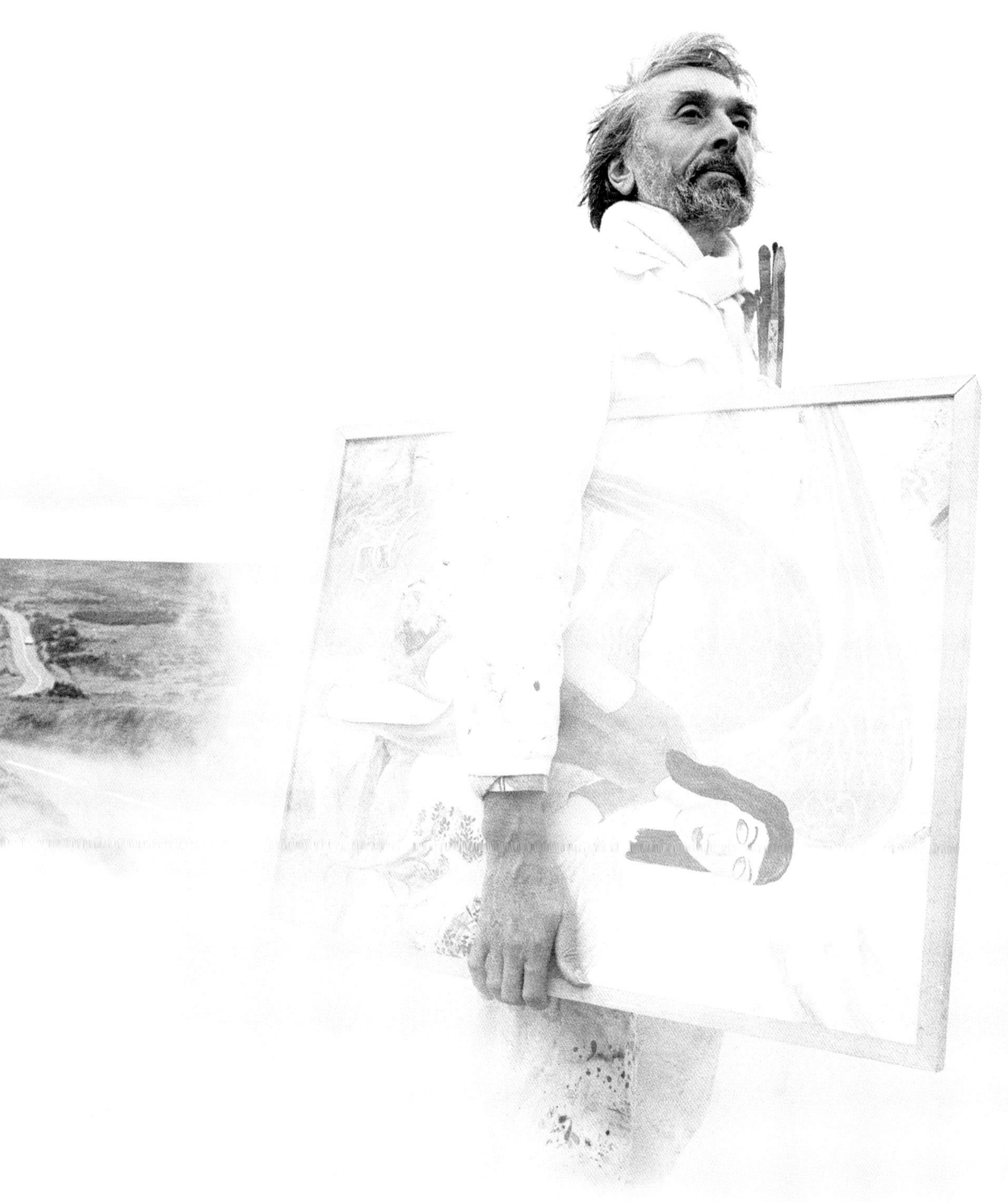

lydia

dans la nuit

"Just say how you engage with life, through the eyes of a potato, on a side of A4."

This divorced, father-of-two is made background to the tuber. It is a constructed iconography. The tuber is made dominant. Why? - because the potato is perceived as a paradigm of the mundane. It is idiomatically used as a neutral carrier of adjectives like "hot" and "couch", yet itself, in journalistic cliché, is always "humble". The viewer (pause, dear reader, and *think* the image) is caught in the semiological denotations and connotations. Through ways of understanding I recognise the danger of being made a prisoner in a mask, although it can be convenient in the processions of life.

The potato in its variety and study is one fascinating route through history and science. In this masquerade I can use the tuber to parade my views by drawing attention to its origins (high life at low latitudes), socio-economic history (e.g. its Spanish discovery in the Andes in 1537 where it had been grown for centuries, European riots in 1848 to 1990s Chinese methods), symbolism (pre-Colombian art and ritual to Nigel Mullan's, 1994 installation *The Potato Gateway*), biology, agronomy and breeding (Scottish 19th C breeders and the Agricultural Improvers to genetic engineering). With degrees in agriculture and ecology (the science *not* the erroneously used, media term), and working experience of farm life in the Lowlands and Highlands of Scotland, including teaching and over thirty summers with the Scottish Department of Agriculture inspecting growing crops of seed potatoes, I became intrigued with crop history especially the lore and history of the potato. Later, travelling for months at a time in Asia, Europe, Africa and Latin America, with a special interest in high altitude, tropical plants, I became fascinated by the sophistication of survival strategies in subsistence farming. Working on archaeological excavations I became particularly interested in how these were used in the past (like memory, history is the original virtual reality). Subsequently I became involved in the identification and interpretation of plant remains from these ancient sites. To place my scientific knowledge in a better context I took another degree in arts and history. Perhaps like Marlowe's *Dr Faustus* "Knowledge it hath ravished me." - my pact with the potato?

I am fascinated by paradox and what the Germans call *verspielt*, in setting ideas against each other in travel and recording programmes for radio. It is the tension we live in, especially as part of the privileged "developed" minority of the world's population, where technical aspiration is now countered by atavistic longings. An industry of romantic idealism has sprung up in which nutritionally unqualified or gullible food journalists pontificate. The "Countryside" becomes an urban myth. It has become an ideal - more an advertiser's concept or a public park. Deviations from this rustic utopia worry urban visitors. The RSPB alone has a well-meaning membership whose *urban* quotient exceeds *total* political party membership in the UK. It has an income over £20m per year and is a substantial landowner itself. Its brief is for the birds and whether employment and good land use is a first principle is debatable.

Scientists are perceived as a fickle priesthood, condemned for making monsters or spoiling muck and mystery "natural" products by analysis and explanation (" E numbers" !) . "Organic" groups claim to have "rediscovered" or "rescued" old potato varieties which are *already* maintained in the most complete collection of potato varieties (700+) in Europe at the Scottish Agricultural Science Agency in Edinburgh - indeed the legal supply of these varieties must originate as healthy, certified stocks from there.

Meaning itself is fudged by the semantic delusion of "political correctness" which too often confuses equality with similarity. A media-fed clamour seems to prevail over the dispassionate analyses of facts. John Lawton summed it up in 1995 "The irony of the information age is that it has given new respectability to uninformed opinion." We are told more youngsters than ever pass higher examinations and that we have more graduates than ever, yet surveys show a greater belief in science fiction television than an understanding of basic biology and statistics.

The potato's neutrality has been compromised by its role in Ireland's famine where it has been blamed rather than Britain's well-documented policy failures of the time and English nationalism requires Raleigh to have introduced the potato rather than its more probable, anonymous introduction by Spanish sailors. The designer, Sir Terence Conran, opened a gourmet restaurant in London and was challenged in 1997 as to the kind of potatoes he used. His spokeswoman said "A potato is just a potato." This must be the ultimate victory of style over substance. A plea - Demand named varieties! They are as different as CAMRA beers and with longer more eventful histories!

David Smith 1998

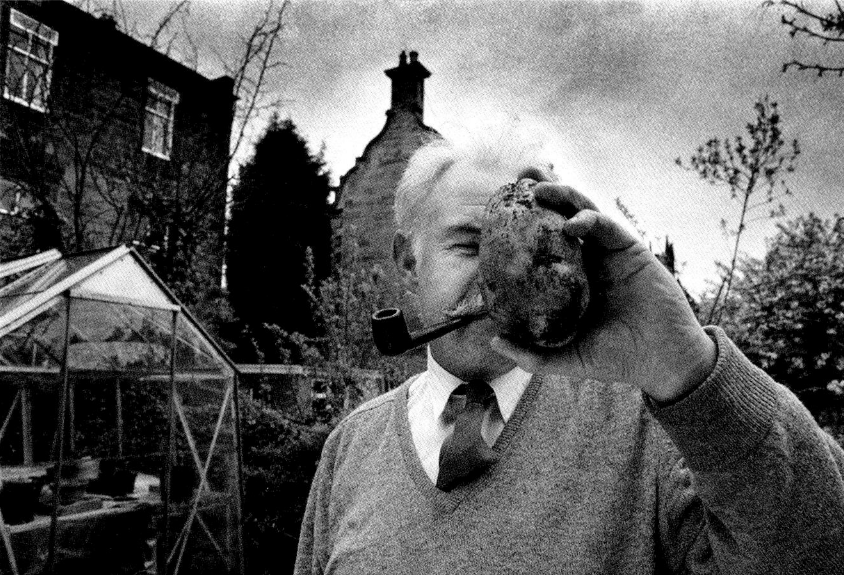

alan fairweather

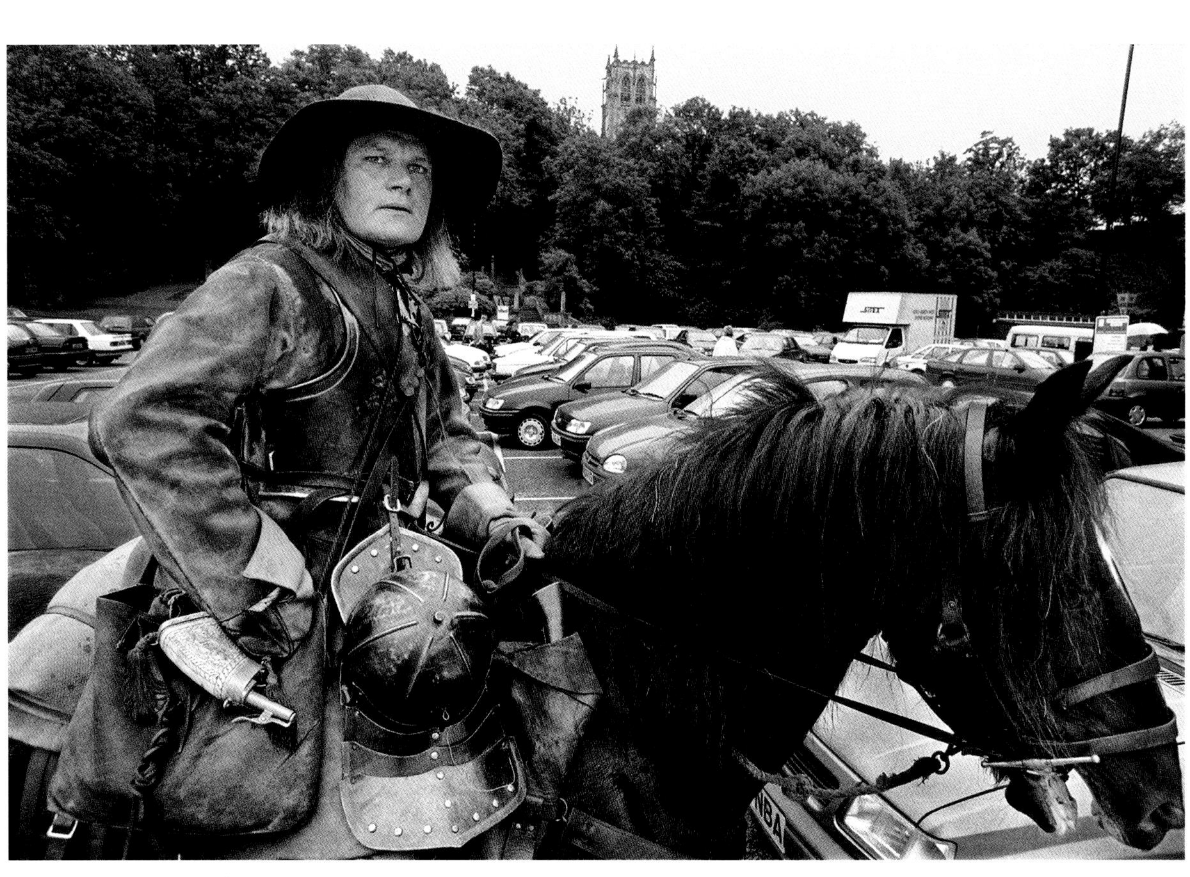

captain helliwell

Captain Helliwell in the 17th century was an officer in Oliver Cromwells roundhead army, fighting against the cavaliers of King Charles 1st. Since those days, however, Helliwells Spirit has evolved to become a Spirit Guide. He is my Spirit Guide and has been so since 1987.

By taking his part, dressing in full milatary uniform of the period, and by riding Oliver my warhorse, I am able to draw down from the astral planes the Captains presence, whereof we commune together. Our partnership manifests itself in so many ways other than my simply riding as a roundhead throughout Yorkshire and Lancashire though. Each year, for instance, I am set various challenges by Helliwell which I must rise to, such as my having to write a book on the civil war in 1993.

Our partnership works both ways. When I become Captain Helliwell, horseriding along the highways, in symbolic terms, in my battledress I am able to take up arms against progress, but in particular that which the Captain and I detest more than words can tell - the dreaded motor car.

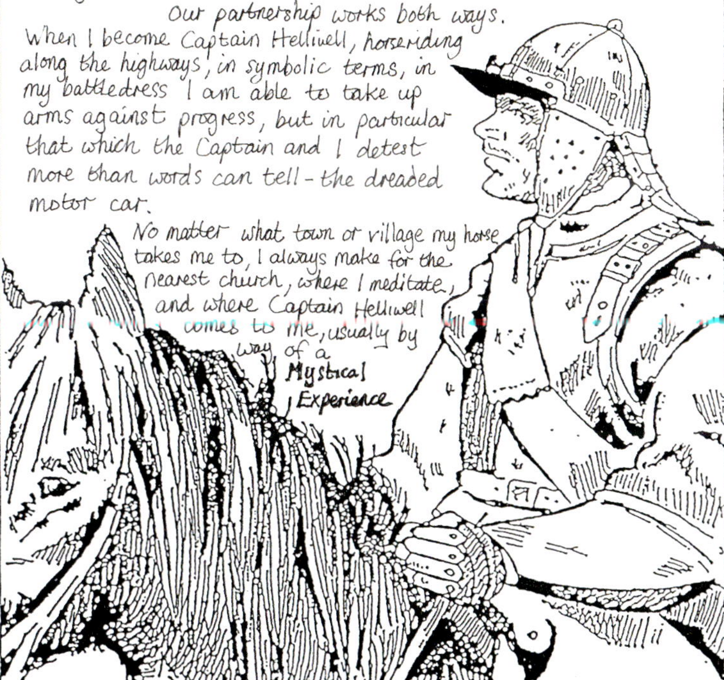

No matter what town or village my horse takes me to, I always make for the nearest church, where I meditate, and where Captain Helliwell comes to me, usually by way of a Mystical Experience

"...but anyhow, I've got more stones around here than just that...

Now, we'll walk up here a little bit. You can see me stone circle in front of you, er, some of the stones here are all sculptured out.

This particular one we're looking at, it's got a (h)eye and a nose and a chin and it looks just like one over in Easter Island, and, er we'll move up a bit farther, now, er, and let me say, in this country to this present day, there is 900 sets of stone circles still remaining... and, there's two types of stone circles.

Obviously one is the type that I've got with the 'centre stone' - that represents man, or a phallus, and the outer circle represents woman, and this particular stone circle, it was like... when you danced in it, it was like a fertility, er, thing. And there 'idden many writers, past or present, would ever doubt they weren't used for dancing.

(In a whispered tone) But there was one story about this stone circle I didn't tell yer. (Swallows) When I was building in 1982, er, people didn't talk much about the stones, it was a bit of closed shop, but I knew that all the stones, most of the stones in Cornwall, had names, so, I thought I'd better give my... my... stone circles some names. So I called them after the ladies in me life, but there were exceptions.

First of all there was me Great Aunty Hilda, cos she was born of seven sisters and I thought there's a bit of luck. Then there was one called Monica, then the next one, we're moving clockwise, er... that was Marjorie after Mother. Then the one down

there in the corner, that one's called The Secret Lady. See, (whispered tone) we had a day out together, me and this woman (car zooms past) we did things we shouldn't do, and (hesitates) when our day had finished, I said,

'Look, I've no money to buy you flowers' but, er (cough) I said, 'Look, I've no money to buy you flowers (swallows) but soon I'm going to build a stone circle and I'm going to put nine or ten tons of granite in the ground and call it after you to celebrate our wonderful day...' (Takes breath)

She said, 'Ed, I think 'tis best to leave me out of it, cos I don't want me husband to find out anything about this.'

So I said, 'All right, to overcome it, we'll call it The Secret Lady' and that's what it's been ever since.

Moving on to the next stone, that one's called Jackie. (In a low voice) Jackie and I had a little romance together and, like, I nearly did run away with her, but I was afraid me uncle would cross me off the will and (long, long, snigger...)

I'm sorry I laugh but this is serious thing. When a man's young he thinks of love but when you get older, it's all about money..."

marjorie

the secret lady

jackie

the peace maker

the moon

monica

marian

aunty hilda

the sun

the judgement stone

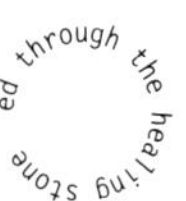

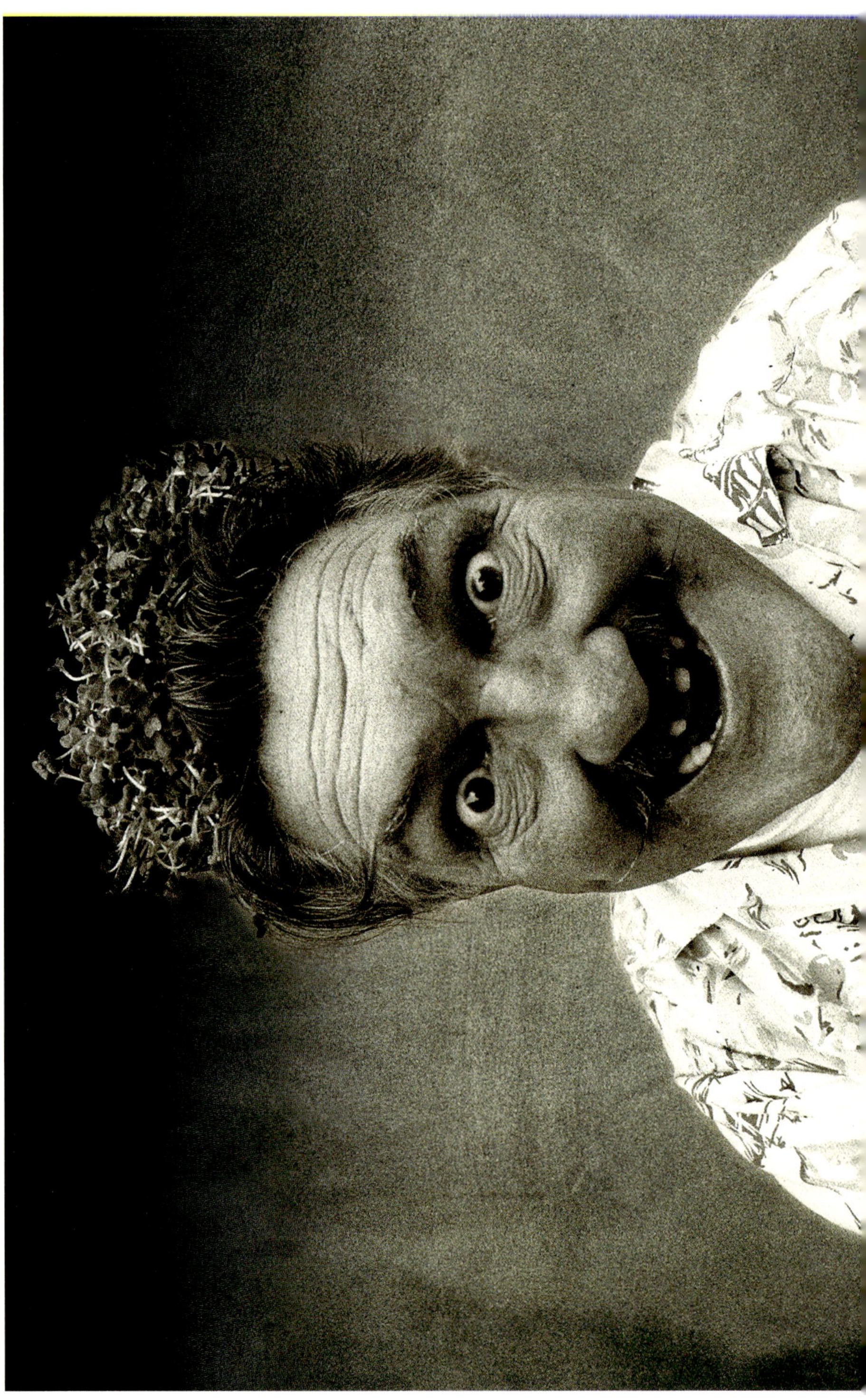

mAd mick

The first unusual thing that I did for charity was to be locked in a public house gents W.C. for four days, the event was very successful, From then onwards my mind never stopped thinking what to do next, very soon I found myself eating nothing but baked beans for a whole week no bread or any other food at all. After this I decided to grow water cress on my head, first it was shaved, then blotting paper that I had started growing cress seeds on was stuck to my bonce, I had to use a special pillow in order to sleep with it on, after a while I had to remove it as the smell it gave out was to much for every-one. Still thinking what to do with my head I decided to have it shaved by a butcher who used his meat cleaver and boning knife, after that I had it pulled out with pincers charging people £1 per tug. My next venture was to grow a radish in my left ear this was achieved by placing a small plastic bag containing compost and radish seed to my ear using plaster to to secure it, this resulted by me getting strange looks as I went about my everyday business. The next stunt was for me to eat twenty raw cloves of garlic a day for a week, I was not very popular, it was a sure way to keep people at bay. I have done numerous other eccentric things, this way of life makes me tick as it gets the tension out of my system, and I intend to go on as long as possible

Mad Mick Summers

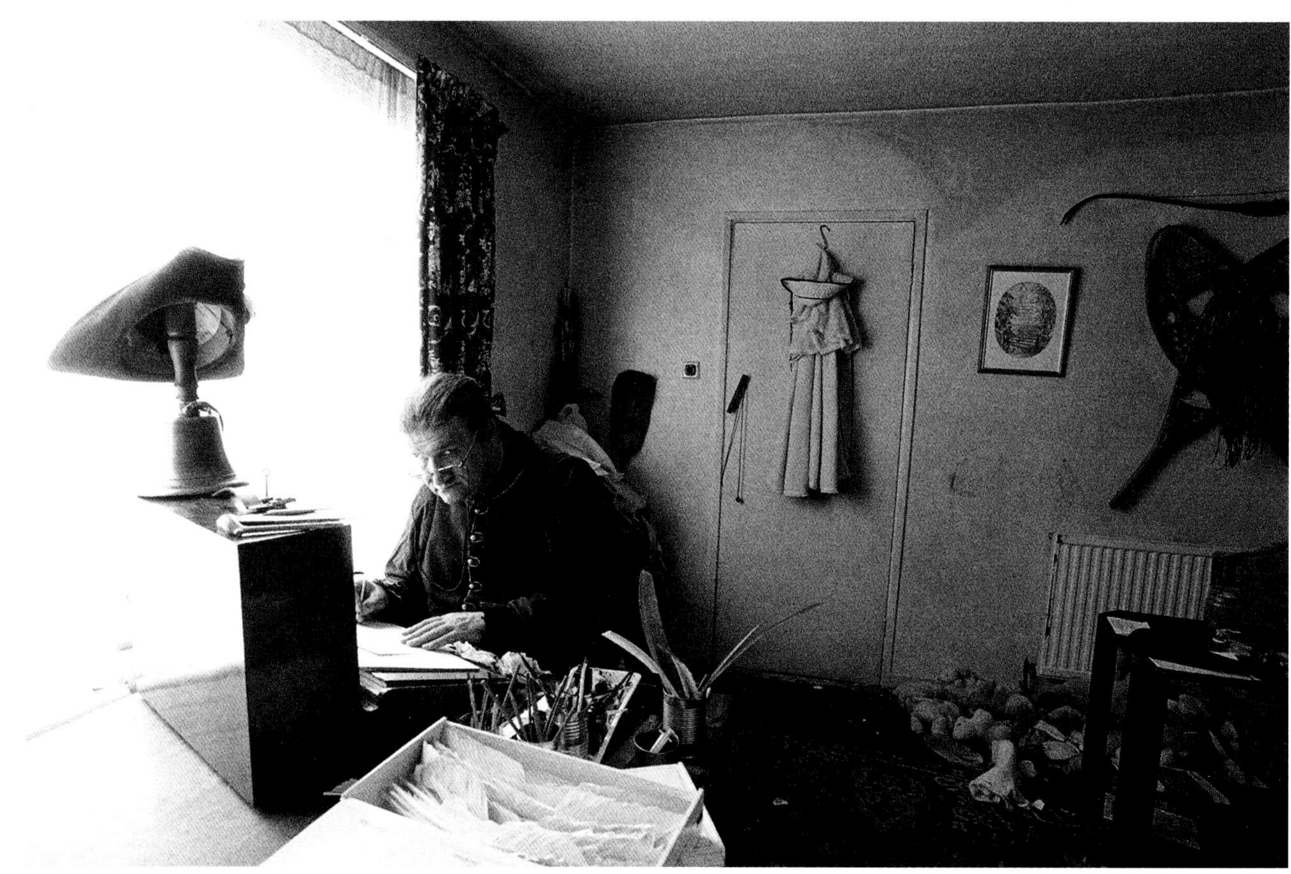

tom clarkson

That which is old, but
still of use, old skills, old
tools, knowledge that has
served for many years,
collected, stored, and
used again when need
arises, the skills kept alive
for future generations,
the past, the present and
the future, knit into one
whole and brought
alive, this, for me, is
history.

Tom Clarkson
Artist - Craftsman
Town Cryer - Historyan.

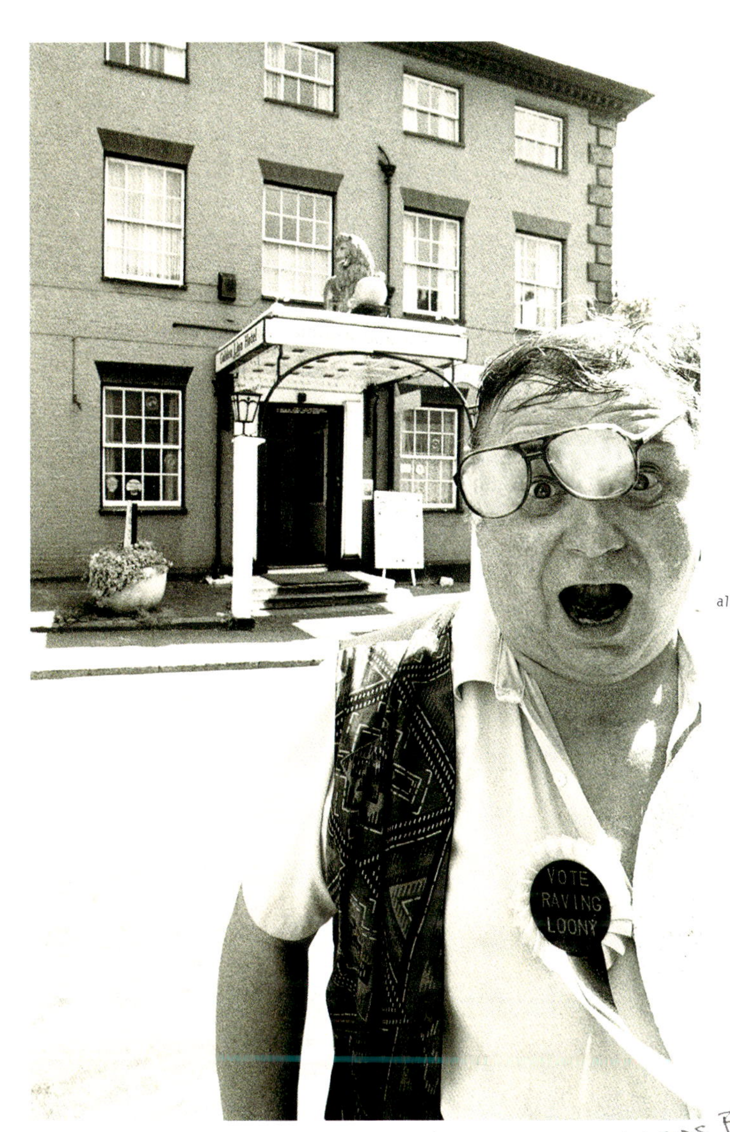

I WAS THE WORLDS FIRST MEMBER OF THE OFFICIAL MONSTER RAVING LOONY PARTY TO HOLD OFFICE. I HAVE BEEN ON THE TOWN COUNCIL OF ASHBURTON IN DEVON FOR THE LAST 9 YEARS FOR THE YEAR MAY 94 - MAY 95 I WAS ELECTED DEPUTY MAYOR. WHEN MY TURN CAME TO BECOME MAYOR, THE TOWN COUNCILLORS MUST HAVE THOUGHT BETTER OF IT, GOT COLD FEET, AND VOTED ME OUT. I AM STILL CHAIRMAN OF THE ASHBURTON TOURIST BOARD TO THIS DAY.

~~FIRST MET~~

I FIRST MET SCREAMING LORD SUTCH IN 1958, WHEN WE WERE BOTH ROCK 'N' ROLL SINGERS ON THE SAME TOURING SHOWS.
WHEN I MOVED TO DEVON IN 1978, (IM ORIGINALLY FROM FARNBOROUGH IN HAMPSHIRE) MYSELF AND MY WIFE NORMA PURCHASED THE GOLDEN LION HOTEL, IN ASHBURTON, AND IMMEDIATLEY IT BECAME THE HEADQUARTERS OF THE PARTY THE REST IS HISTORY, THE FUTURE REMAINS FULL OF LOONYISM.

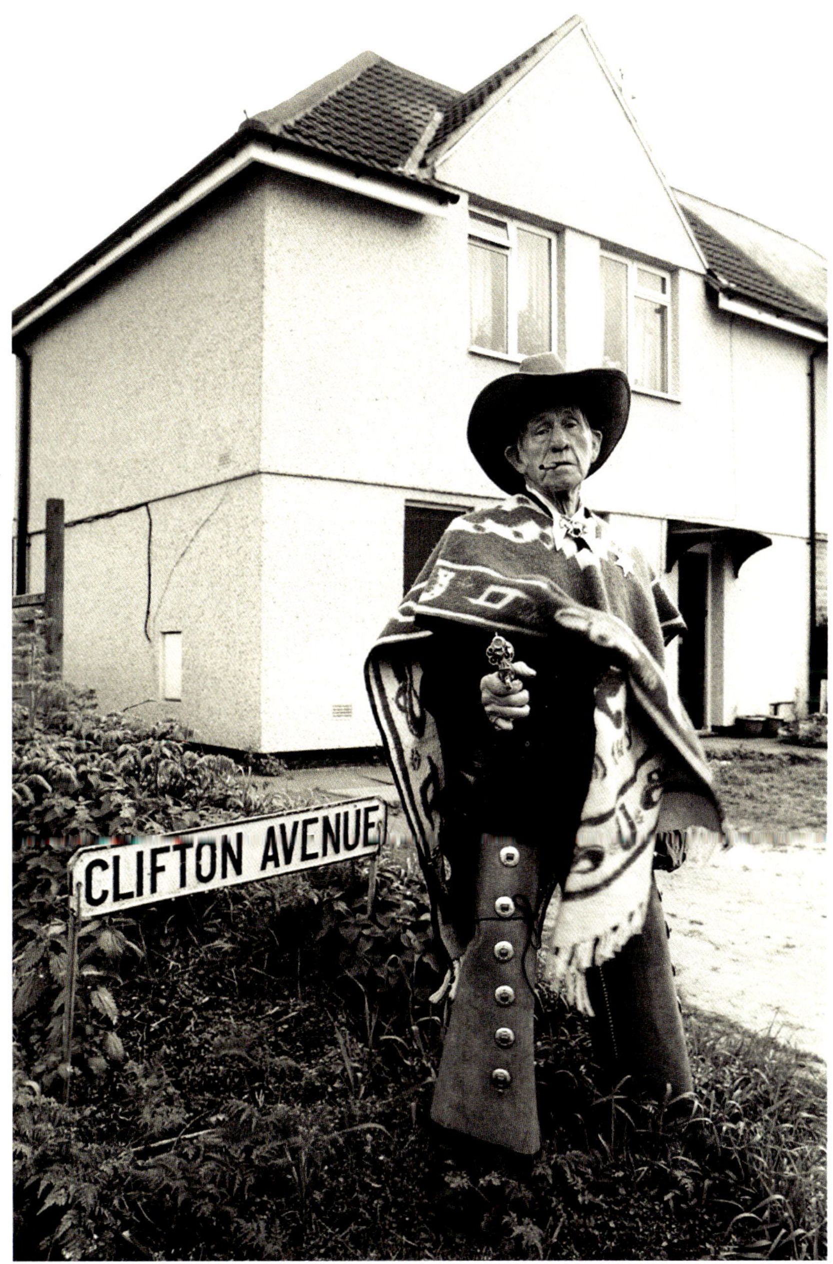

clint eastwood

jake the rake
jake the rake jake the rake

jake the rake

jake the rake

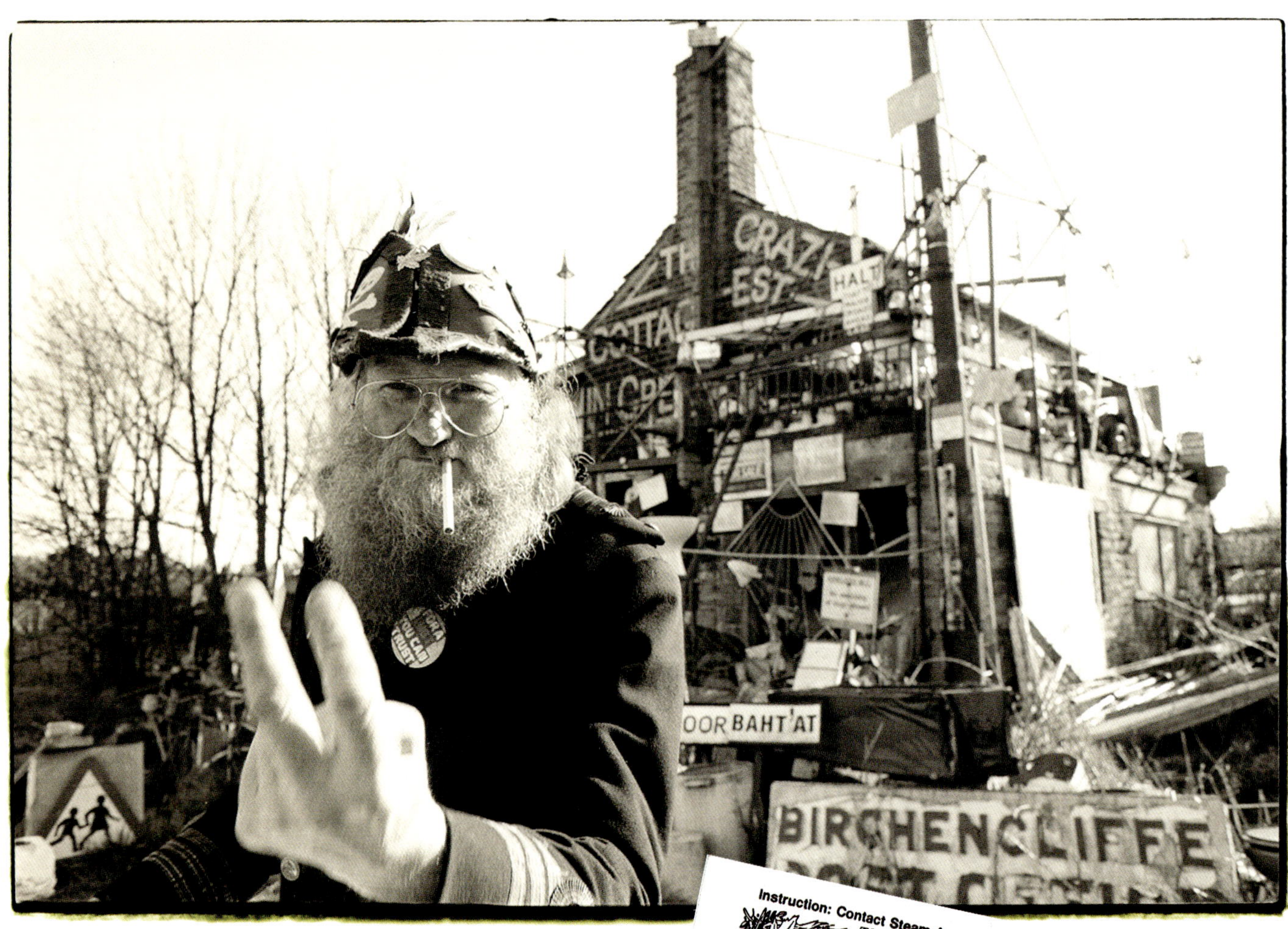

Instruction: Contact Steam-Age Yorkshireman (below) by Telephone/ Snail Mail only
The Cruellest and most Dangerous Animal on Earth is Man
The Most Plentiful Things on Earth: Human Stupidity, Ignorance, Delusion
Beware of Doctors, Lawyers, Politicians and Clergy: Deceivers all

Established 1978
Occasional Bizarre Star
of Radio, Telly & Press Gang.
Hi-Tec Jake on Wurzel Website
Royal Appointments by Telephone only:
HUDDERSFIELD 01484 647103, Night or Day
www.theoccupier.free-online.co.uk
Dear Sir or Madman - Welcome to my world
introducing A Battered and Tarnished Knight of this Realm, but Thinker:

The House of Many Wonders & Kingdom Unique,
(National Monument - 'Wunderful Wurzel-Land'),
The Palace of Poles Apart in Peace Pond Hamlet,
Sallie Nookie at The Edge of Lindley Moor Baht 'at,
Within the Parish Boundary of Longwood Singh in
Ye Ancient Borough of Huddlesfield   HD3 3UA,
Yorkshire Pudding in Once Precious Olde Englande,
Lunatic Asylum of the Accursed Federation of Europe.

Sir Thomas Henry Erasmus Occupier (T.H.E.O. The Ungodly)

Formerly Prof. Jake Jonathan Zebedee Mangle-Wurzel, Lord Longwood Singh etc.
Town Clown of Huddlesfield & King of the Eccentrics by Global Renown.
Obsessional Heretic, Bloody Donor and Sheep-Shagging Champion of all England.
Bard & Squire O' Lindley Moor Baht 'at, Ph.D., A.M.I.Mech.E., E.E.C., Genius, etc.

Tired and Retired Builder of Exquisite Garden Follies and Farmhouse/Cottage Restorations.
Now Hon. Vice President, Chairman & Managing Director of the Benevolent Big Plastic Dildo Co.
Researcher/Writer and Scholar, Community Entertainer and Self-Appointed Ornamental Hermit.
Weaver of Legends, Teller of Tales, Occupational Liar and Imposter, but Seeker After The Truth.
Denouncer of Professional Hypocrites, Atheist, Misanthrope, and Precious Bane of Inhumanity.
Misogynistic Husband of Many Weird Wives, and Father of Sir Emmanuel (Manoyle) Ramsbottom.
Manoyle died 1996. Jake is now father of Princess Pips and Grandfather of Sir Shatt.
A Willie-Wag with only 3 vices - Talking, Smoking and Total Self-Indulgence. Have a Nice Day. Thank you & Goodnight.
Newsflash: Kirklees Candidate for 1996 'Hon. Members Brown Underpants Party'
From 1999 Jake became serious geneologist and romantic match-maker

I am Indebted to Sir Allan Grainger for allowing my Character,
Sir Cedric Centrefold, to Grace his Photographic Work "I AM."
His book had better be a Masterpiece of Its Kind, and This of Mine a tiny Tour-de-Force. But how can
Anyone compress into a Single A4 an Analytical Thesis on Human Existence, including One's Own Life?

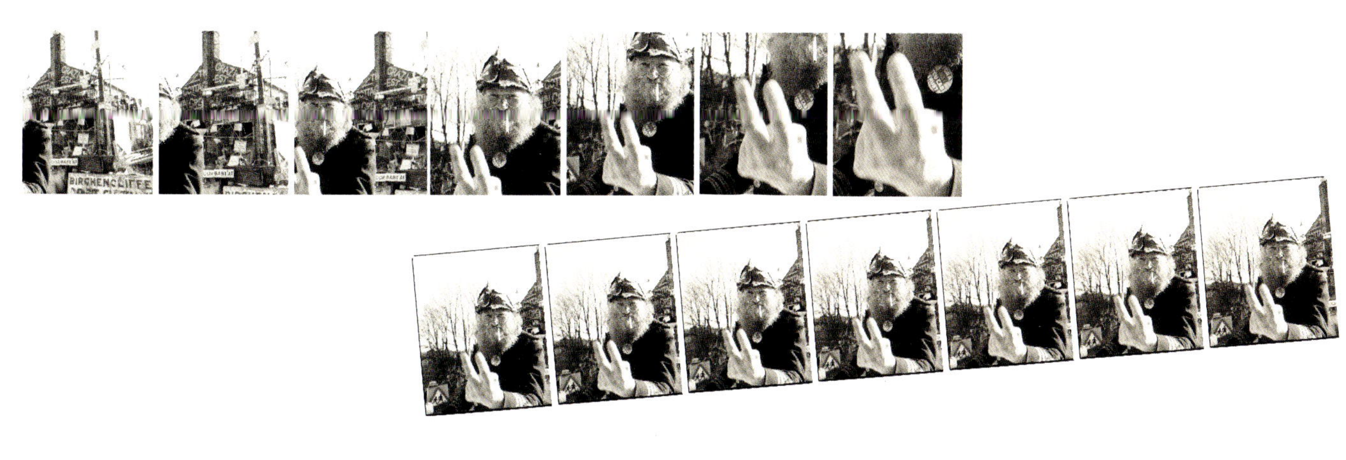

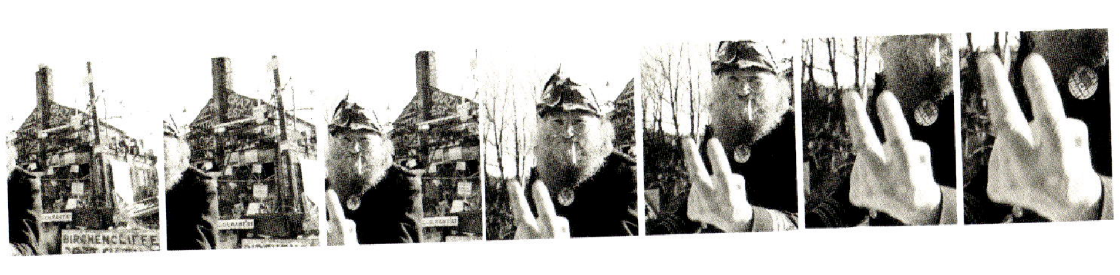

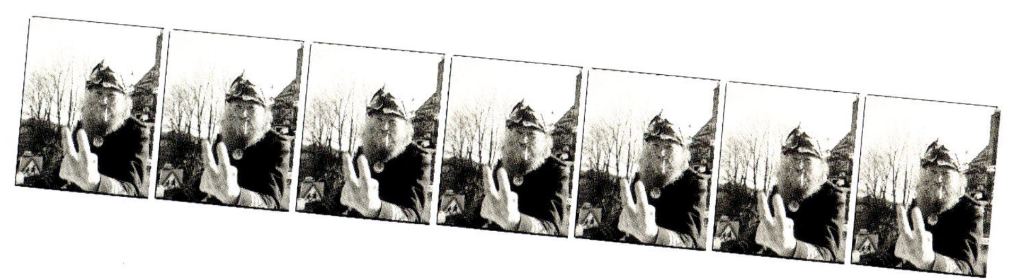

The Wise Words of 'Desiderata' should be nailed up Everywhere On Earth, yet Life has distorted a few
Unmellow Fellows toward Cynical Misanthropy, contemptuous of their own Disgraceful Species.
Now Public Hermit of 'Lindley Moor Baht'at', my Character was once renowned as Joker Jake Mangle-Wurzel,
Crazy Clown of Huddlesfield Town, in Yorkshire Pudd. Both Garrulous Wag and Serious Constructive Artist,
this Agitating Heretic and Rebel presently Promulgates a Savage Satire which Few can Recognise or Comp-
-rehend.

Hoho Sapiens is the Cruellest and Most Dangerous Animal on Earth - Human Stupidity, Ignorance,
and Delusion our Most Plentiful Ingredients. Beware of Doctors, Lawyers, Politicians and The Clergy -
Professional Deceivers All - let alone Conventional Criminals. It has fallen My Duty to Discover and to
Express the Obscure Facts of Life - as I perceive them - especially Fallacy and Misrepresentation.
Philosopher and Moralist, Michel de Montaigne (1533-'92) spent Many Years in the Study of Human Nature,
concluding that, so confusing were the Contradictory Elements, only Divine Revelation could Reveal the
Truth. Ah, 'The Truth', so often a Matter of Opinion! Then 'God' is so obviously the Concoction of Man,
Endowed with Our Own Image, Nature and Ideals, the only Miracle Appearing to Me is that So Many Simple-
-tons can Believe such Pabulum, then call it Fact and Truth. Holey Baloney, Me Lud!

Disorganised Christianity is the Biggest Hoax and Swindle ever Perpetrated on, and Willingly Swallowed
by, Countless Deluded of Our Ludicrous Species. A Crutch for them who think they need it and Refuse to
Die! Religious Belief is for those unable to accept the Harsh Realities of the Only Life, & Only World
of which we have any Knowledge or Proof. O how Hope doth Triumph over Experience.

It is unnecessary that Man should comprehend his One Great Imponderable - The Creation. Following
that, Ingenious Scientists have Demonstrated the Composition, Evolution and Function of Our Universe.
We have Everything We Need in Nature, without resorting to the Supernatural. Rationalistic Education &
Secular Humanism are of the Greatest Importance and the Way Forward for Mankind, though we are not too
far from Self-Destruction. Most folk fail to accurately assess Humanity, Life and Death, using only a
Small Proportion of Potential Intellect. O what a Backward Species we truly are, Programmed with Medio-
-crity, from Cradle to The Grave.

My Own Speciality - Authentic, Deeply-Rooted, Creative Eccentricity - is Misconstrued by Some of the
Ignorant as Stupidity, Futility or Mental Illness. They cannot have read the Many Enlightening & Enter-
-taining Works which Illustrate the Opposite. My Own Character and Performance are too Contradictory to
be Accurately Analysed by any other person than My Own Goodself, yet I get Properly Pissed-Off when Un-
-der-estimated, Misconstrued and Misrepresented (often deliberately) even after using Plain English and
Obvious Ridicule. For anyone interested, I was found under a Guzbery Bush, the 20th Day of Merry May -
in 1938 - the Middle of Five Offsprings to a Grossly Incompatible Couple. Nature and Nurture Wrought-
about the Perverse, Ambivalent, Enigmatical, Cack-handed, Social Oddity which 'I AM'. My Sincere Apolo-
-gies to The World!

Much of John Gray's Conventional Life went Down The Drain toward the End of 1977...
Stubbornly refusing to Surrender to the Slings and Arrows, he set about 'The Making of Mangle-Wurzel',
a Life-Saving Enterprise, into the Euphoric Spring of '78, quite unable to Predict the Bizarre Consequ-
-ences.

Ingenious Joker Jake then Ploughed His Own Furrow, entertaining Himself deliberately & the Rest
of The World by a Fluke! His Versatile Career became Relatively Renowned, for Selective Interest. He
Circumnavigated the Globe without leaving England, while the World came Trickling to His Kingdom Come.
From 1989, He was Declared 'Le Roi des Excentriques', in Many Other Tongues too. Ah, Success at Last!!!

'It is a Mistake to suppose that Men succeed thro' Success - they much oftener Succeed thro'
Failure'.

Something similar happened with the Extraordinary Twice-Rich, Twice-Ruined, Joshua Abraham Norton - (1819-'80) the London-Born, Self-Elected 'Emperor of the United States', a Giant among Eccentrics, who remains an Enigma to This Day. Yet, at this Moment of Publication, Professor Wurzel will have Reigned over 'Wunderful Wurzel-Land' for longer (and still going strong) than Norton 'Ruled' his Very Different Realm - 20 years and 113 Days. Jake also became a Groaning Grand-Paps to His Daughter Pipkins' Immacul- -ate Misconception (Shamus Matt) - another Inherited Cock-Up.

My Joyful Indebtedness to Dear Mother's Scholarly, Atheistic, Eccentric Grandfather, George Thomas Whitehead (1853-1933) whose Precious Writings I discovered in 199?. They helped me to cast off the Last Vestiges of Religious Indoctrination, enabling the Clear-Sighted Message since Preached from 'Pulpit on the Roof', to both four and Two-legged Sheep in the Fields below. Alas, very few of Man defeat Hypocrisy.

When the Moment is Right, I'll enjoy Burying Myself in 'Two Ton o' Good Stiff Watter-Prufe Concrate', in the Mechanised Garden Tomb, Long-prepared & Waiting. Hands Off, you Obscene Pathologists, Interfering Coroners and Vulturine Funeral Directors. The INDIVIDUALIST'S DEATH & BURIAL are Too Precious to entrust to Unimaginative Servants of the State. Only a Brave & Chosen Few will Dare Attend Rebellious Entombing.

My Heartfelt Appreciation & Love to those Goodfriends & Suzie True, who cont'd to Care for This Codger despite His Many Egocentrical Exasperations. Have a Drink on ME You Lot, but be sure ter Buy Yer Own.... (Oh Yes, I'm a Mean Bugger too!). Thankyou for Thinking and Goodbye. Finished This Last Day of Year 1999.
Composed While of Sound Mind but Dubious Boddy by Sir Thomas Henry Erasmus Occupier, T.H.E.O.the Ungodly, Jake the Rake, Longwood Singh, Miss Gorjuss Gladyss, H.R.H. Ye Holey Verjin Mary-Anne Shufflebottom, etc.

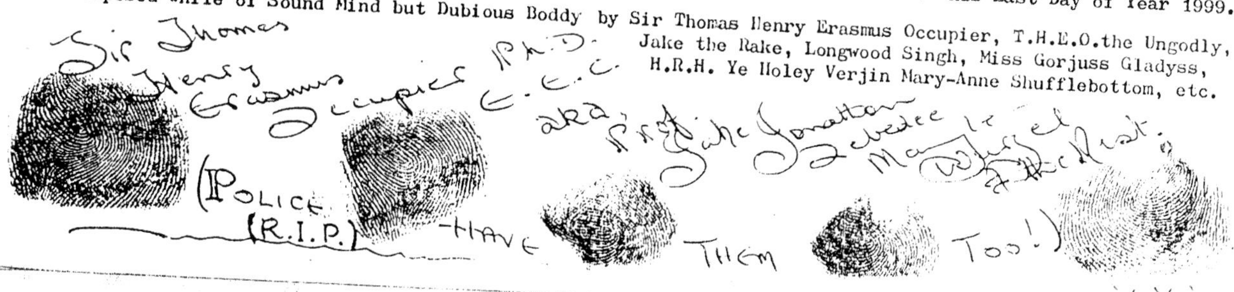

250 word s for ALAN GRAINGER's   book.   01273 700612

LORD TIVERTON HOWELL

Being left at a chip shop by my daddy at 12 years of age with only a suitcase, presented me
with a splendid chance to work out life for myself!   Education finished I started work at 14.

My claim to fame is I that I have never been 'taught' anything by anyone since 12 years of age.

Fortunately I had the dual gifts of, splendid powers of observation, and, a clear way of
thinking . The luck was that I escaped being 'educated' by tutors foisting re-cycled
information   onto me. **I progressed by observation and experience.**

Two careers. The first, was through metal work, into electronics, then product design - hi-fi,
office telephones, language laboratory's, electro-medical devices - and finally car building
industrial robots. As Chief Engineer, Head of Design for a Hawker Siddeley Division the
going was tough, and I thought I had topped out - so I resigned.

Career two.   I sold the house and put the £4,500 into building a Health Food shop, living
above. After teaching myself the business my son and I opened 25 more in the next 5 years
- without borrowing!   After a three year holiday I came back to float the Company but
Holland and Barrett gave us £3,100,000 cash, for what were now 50 shops/restaurants and
saved us the bother.

Easy peasy.

I now above another shop in the centre of Old Hastings in my version of a Loony Lords
Folly.   A bizarre but very liveable pad with indoor swimming pool and personal elevator.
It's open to the public once a year for charity.

I was lucky to escape being educated.

283 words - sorry.

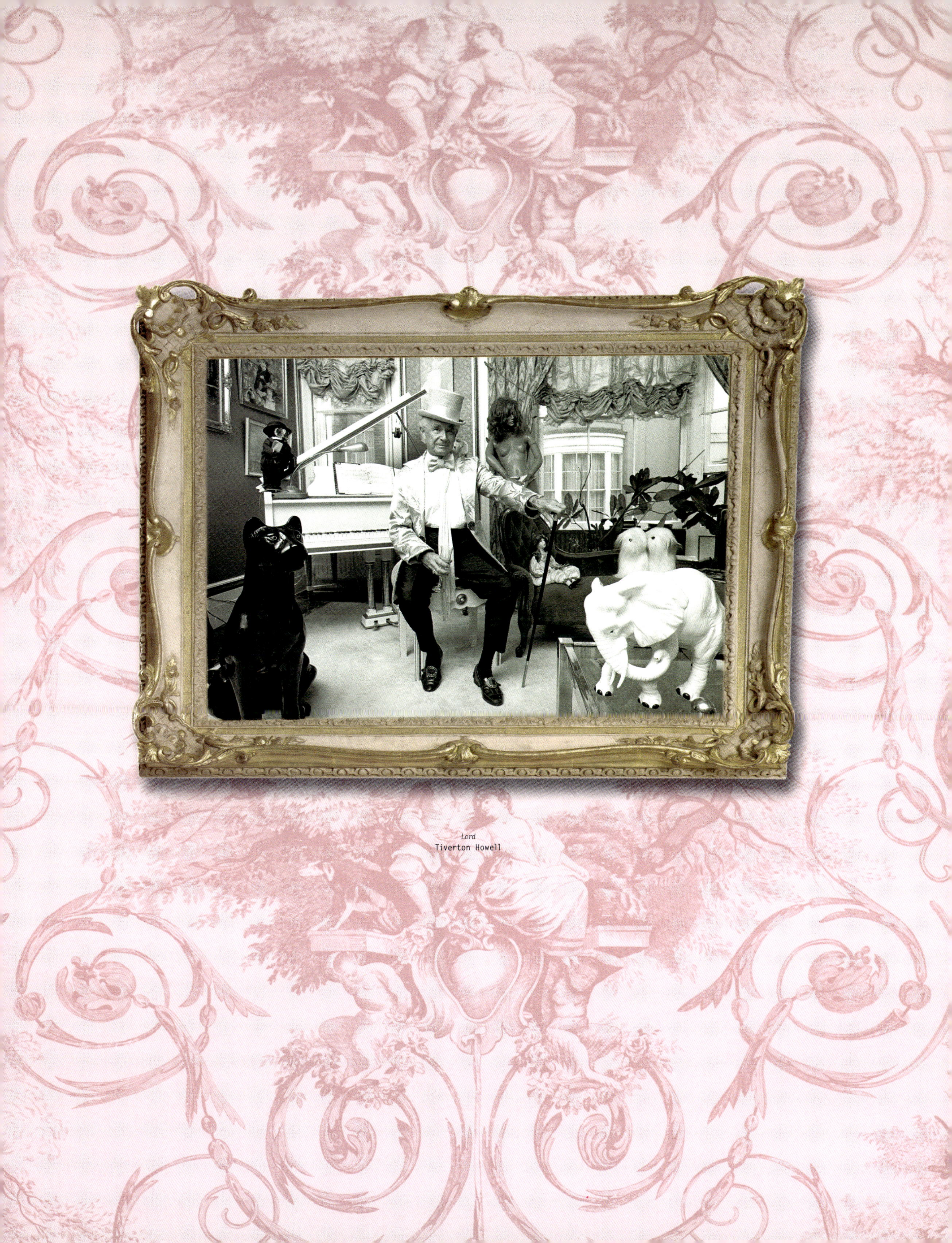

Lord
Tiverton Howell

I NEED NO CHURCHES,

I NEED NO ORGANS.

I NEED NO STAINGLASS WINDOWS

THE BREEZE GIVES ME THE MUSIC
I NEED

THE SUN GIVES ME ALL THE
COLOURS I WANT

THE GREAT SPIRIT MAKES
EVERYTHING IN A QUIET WAY

HOPE THIS WILL DO

KEEP WELL

C.B

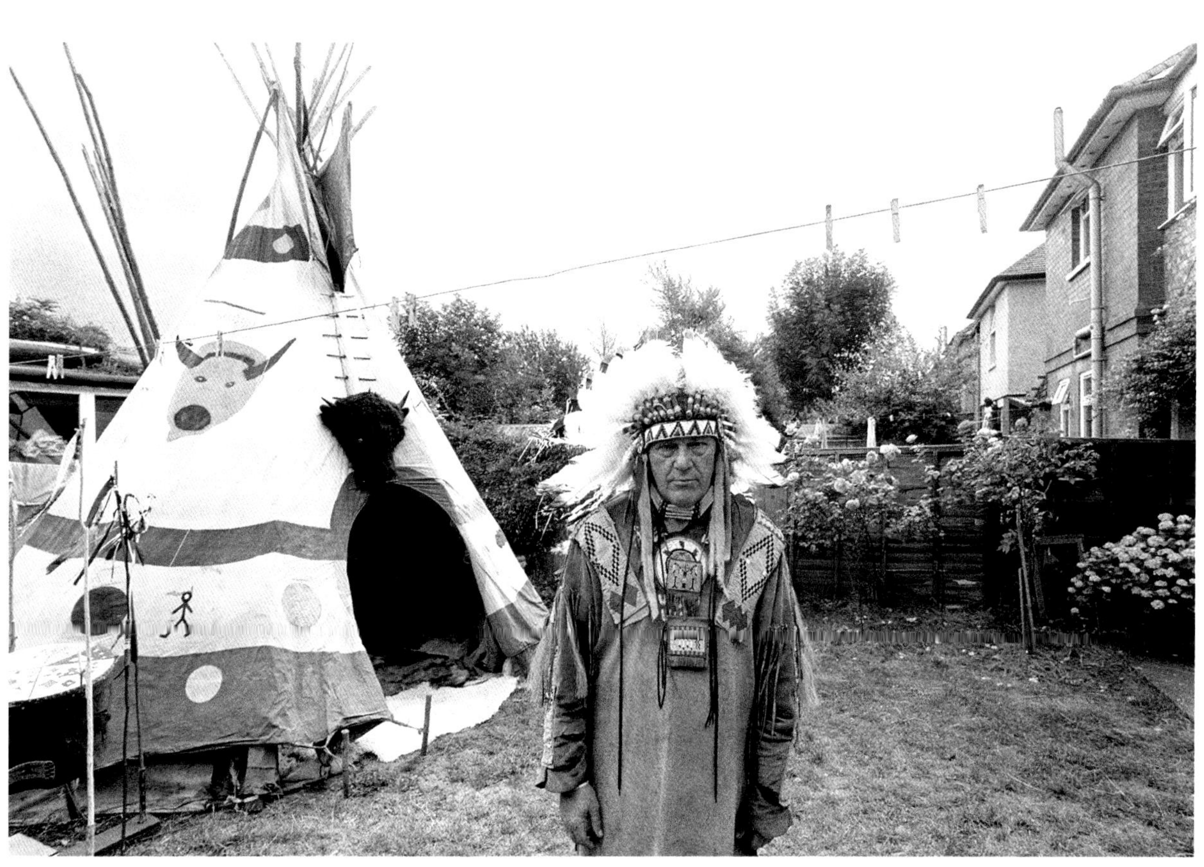

crazy buffalo

John Slater.

I was born in I937 in South Africa where my parents divorced too quickly
for me to know the joys of ha ving my nappy changed by my father.
My mothe r returned to the home of her mother in Liverpool and went out
to work to support us all.
The war years came and lots of houses went (in a cloud of bomb smoke) but
I don't recall fear, per se, just a desire for peace and quiet!
My mother re-married and my new Step-Father decided my sister and I should
go to 'good' boarding schools. I hated every minute of my time at school
and found little to hold my attention academically. The results, after
becoming a fine boy sopra no with a flair for writing poetry, was that my
final school report had my learned Step Fa ther fuming, 'What the bloody
he ll are we going to do with a singing poet??!
My natural instincts seemed decidedly eccentric. I spent days 'underground'
in home made 'Ca ves' and 'dens' and the solitary hours spent in such
bizarre situa tions helped me to develop a strong attachment to nature,
ha rmony of thought and a very pronounced un-materialistic philosophy.
In turn over the years I became a Royal Marine Commando, a window cleaner,
lorry driver, waiter, steward on a luxury yacht, Social worker, salesman,
timber ja ck, cave man, public speake r, marathon walker, tour guide,
security gua rd, dog lover, humanist, driftwood artist and all manner of
interesting ave nues opened up to me as I sought my 'inner' and real self.
The importance of seeing as many points of the compass of life as possible
doesn't fade but latterly my interests have developed considerably on
matters of spiritual, physical and mental well being, particularly as I
have experienned four heart attacks, three 'out-of-body' scenarios and
still, to this day, have NO idea as to just who I really am!
I do know however, what I am.

One human being, ever eager to re-polish his 'L' plates and to go on
'experiencing' the education of this incredible life journey. Nothing
stays the same for any of us and all tha t we can learn here must surely
lead to a kind of 'graduation', a triumph of self realisation that opens
up like a sea view as fog lifts from still grey waters.
Other lives beckon: other lessons approach in other time scales.
No mortal man has eve r existed outwith his own unfolding karma. No man
should eve r believe he is exempt from the timeless rules of the
pe rfe ction of the primordial vibrations.   All his thoughts will
determine all his actions, good or bad.   Where that leaves me I don't
know but learning to be a better person, to give rather than to selfishly
take, to laugh rathe r than cry, to share anything and everything that
co mes through as a caring thought must surely be the highest of ideals.

    Spiritual realisation gained here and now is the most important goal
and that's the only piece of luggage you can expect to take on the next
'trip' with you, so brace yourself Slate r, you're on your way!!

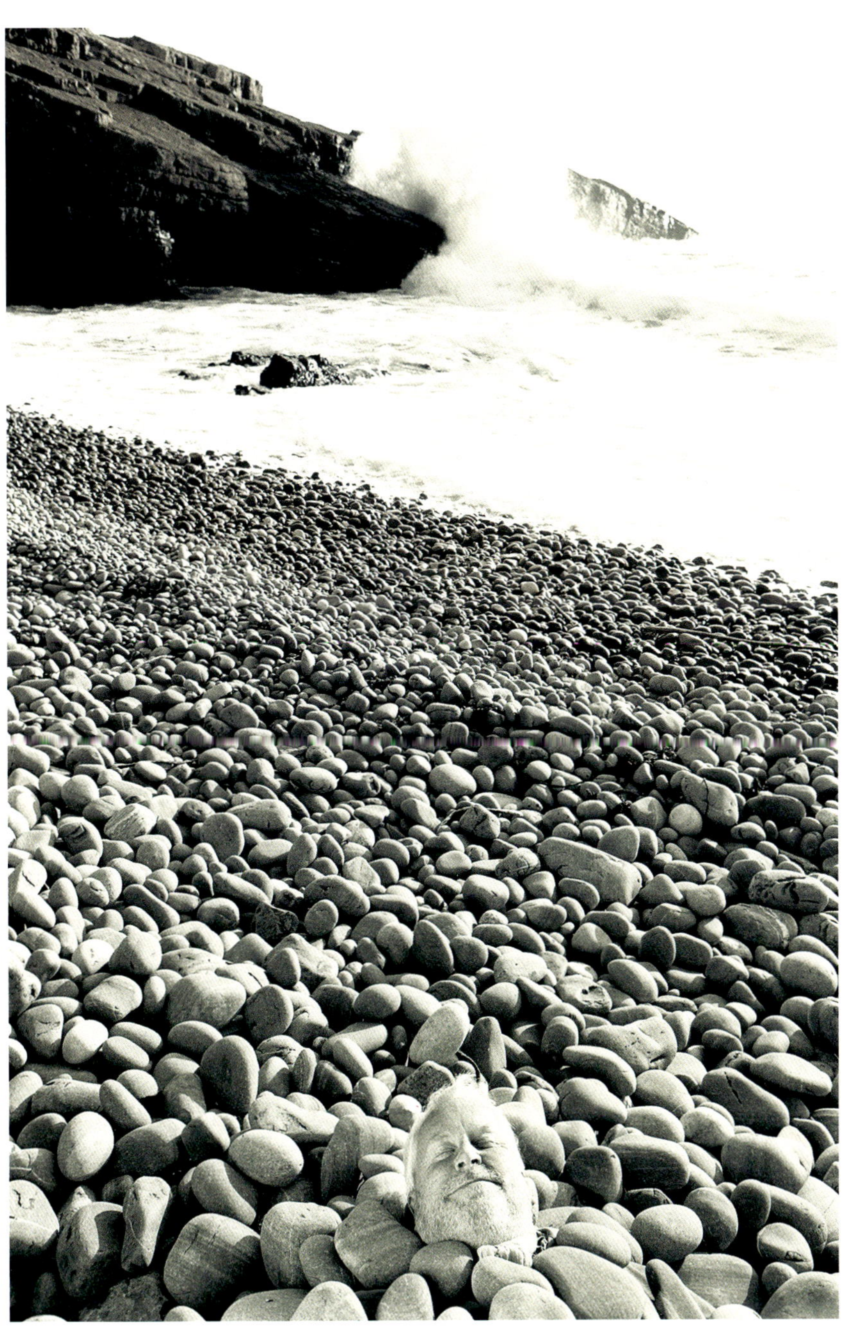

john slater

1/ Allan's photograph taken in 1996 depicts me with Siegfried my personal gnome or nature spirit (who I sculpted into physical existence in 1978) meditating on the painting I was currently creating celebrating the joy of listening to the song of a wren.

2/ To start at a beginning...as a student I attended Brighton College of Art for 4 years, then meriting a place to continue painting at The Royal Academy Schools in London for a further 3 years. At The Schools I met Ron Atkin a fellow student. We married in 1960. We have 2 sons. In 1970 we came to live in North Devon, hoping both of us to live by painting....

3/ Now to the nitty gritty and to my gnomish revelation... I have never found any difficulty in having an orgasm during sex and as I said we have 2 wonderful now grown up sons. What I discovered in 1978 was that sex is not solely a pleasurable activity, not solely for having children, not even solely for sharing love with one's partner, but it is also a time when, using the mind's inner eye, one can truly create. I write this because I want to share this discovery with as many young people as I can.

4/ From the day I first saw gnomes my whole life changed. Because of what they showed me from a hitherto part of my unconscious mind, I knew I had a lot of inner visualising and exploring in the inner Cosmos to do before I would be able to create paintings which could be of any real consequence.... In the meanwhile it was of the utmost importance to share the gnomes with other people...And so The Gnome Reserve was born - and although in it's infancy, 8,000 people made the journey to our spot in the wilds of North Devon to visit it in it's first year in 1979. It has since been featured in TV on 40 different programmes in GB and abroad and numerous times on radio, in newspapers, magazines and books worldwide.

5/ At the same time, during my sex life I made trees, I made flowers, I made birds, and in my inner being I lived among these creations. I also thus learnt through my inner being of the wonderful diversity and interdependence of external Nature...and all this too needed to be shared - and so The Wild Flower Garden became an integral part of the - thus enlarged to 4 acres - Gnome Reserve. Today in this garden there are about 300 different labelled species of wild flowers, herbs, grasses and ferns and because of all this diversity it attracts many insects, small animals, butterflies and my special joy very many birds both resident and migratory. Visitors say it is a bit of heaven on earth. I like to think and in fact I know that it inspires other people to make wild gardens in which a whole diversity of species can live in little oasis's of full green life amid the prevalent "distorted" monoculture of today.

6/ When people visit The Gnome Reserve and Wild Flower Garden - since 1980 25,000 to 35,000 have visited annually - I like to lend everyone a gnome hat so that regardless of age, sex, nationality, occupation etc etc, everyone can temporaly beome a gnome - which is of course equally 100% humorous.... so the 4 acres is filled with laughter (and for those who wish an exuse/ a way to see external Nature as if newly created/ for the first time through the eyes of a gnome. Whichever way it is an escape from the pressures of life and an entry into the "real" world as Nature made it)

7/ I believe every single person on our planet has within their mind a gnome / the gnomic shaping/forming ability with which to make the life forms which inhabit their own individual psyche and contribute to the collective psyche of mankind. By consciously creating within this inner life I believe we each transform an activity which can be the lowest into one that becomes the highest.. It is interesting to note that the shape of a gnome's hat is the same as the Cosmic cone.

8/ For myself, after years of journey work in my mind's eye - which reflected physically into the creation of The Gnome Reserve and the Wild Flower Garden, the gnomes expanded my consciousness creatively out into the Cosmos, and gave me my personal crock of inner gold at the end of the rainbow....For the JOY that I found at the top of the Cosmic cone with Ron during sex, once found, permeated into everything in life everyday and is a source of inspiration which will never run dry - colouring and freeing my perception of the most simple events in the natural world and everybody I meet into an everlasting source of inspiration for paintings - which I am as equally compelled to attempt to share with people as The Gnome Reserve and Wild Flower Garden.

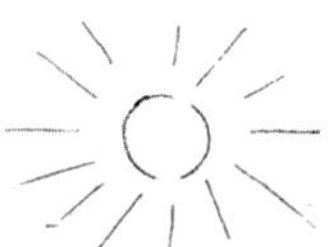

The paintings are organic abstract celebrations including figures of men, women and children flowing in (often rainbow coloured) psychic energy - portrayed by thousands of interlocking shapes.

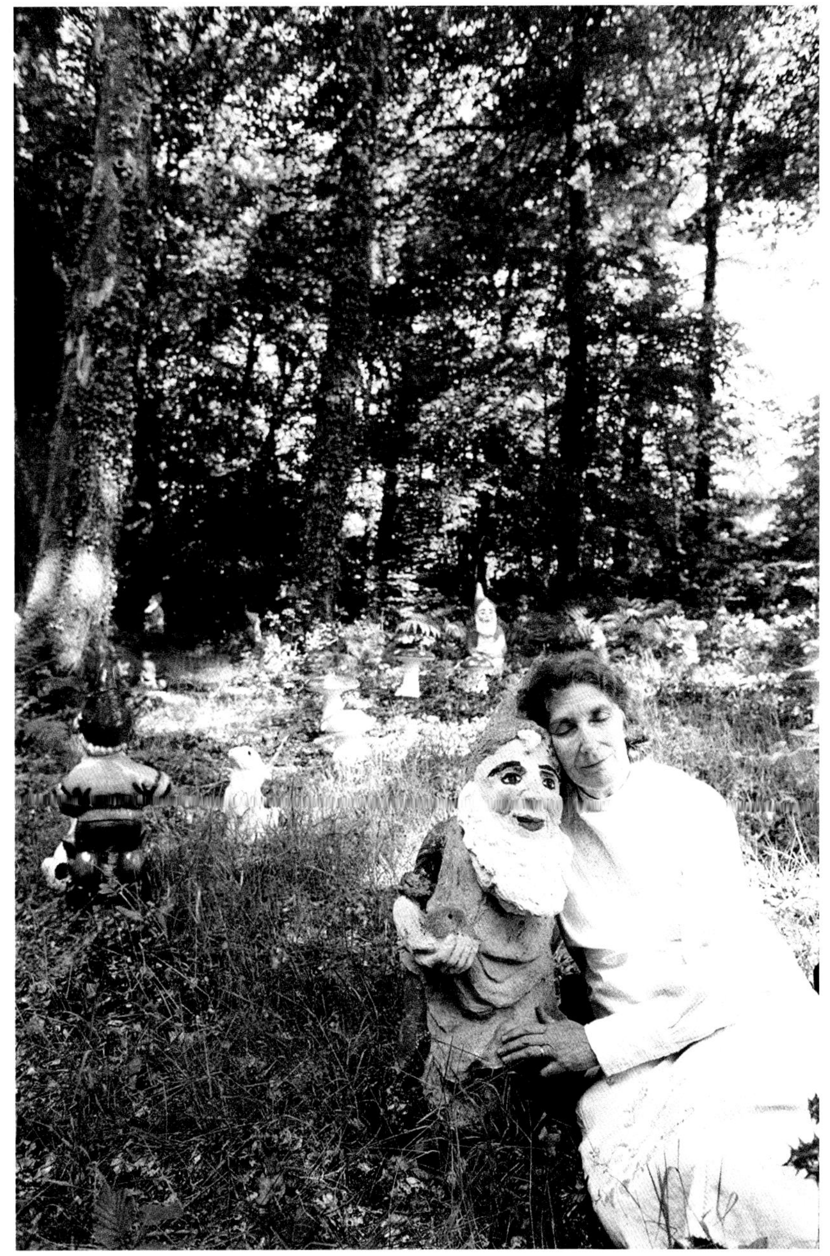

siegfried & ann

Who's normal? Who's not?
Most people think that they know an eccentric when they see one:
it's anyone who is sufficiently different to us that they make us feel uncomfortable.
We try to pigeon-hole them, but we can't; so they make us question ourselves
and the way we live.
The 20 people featured here certainly defy our conventions
by their interests, their lifestyles,
their attitude, the things they say.
Whether they are eccentric is a matter of definition.
They have the confidence and self-belief to do what they want, to say who they are.

Are they mad?
Or is everyone else?

antony woodward

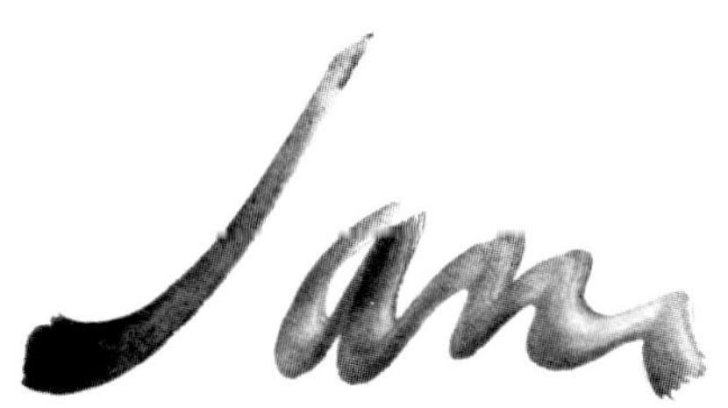

richard booth

Richard Booth asked for your passport

Twenty five years ago.

He wanted Hay-on-Wye

To be an independent place.

Imagine

A state

Where the principle commodity

Is bookshops

Heaven.

alan fairweather

Thanks Alan
I will never take the potato for granted again.

See his text for more details.

bodger

A damp dank pathway that leads up a steep incline into the wood; Bodger's wood.

A place he knows intimately; every tree; every clearing.

For me the wood has an eerie mood to it, and a timeless quality, that unsettles.

The wood is over six hundred years old.

The wood is Bodger's home.

alan hope

Lunacy takes over
In September
In Ashburton
In Devon
All Lunes gather for the Party Conference.

Wonderful proposals are voiced
ie. dog food with special illuminating properties
that make dog turds glow in the dark.

Alan Hope and friends show us it's not bad to be
mad
So give them your support
Lobby now
Britain needs them.

Sitting in his tent, deep in the wood, drinking tea made from rainwater, he tells me
about his life.

A life struggling to preserve a way of looking after woods.

A bodger's way.

Bodger n. a skilled workman.

king arthur

He is the knight
Who protects the land
Who has entered into
A never ending battle.

To stand with Arthur at Stonehenge
Is enough.
No audio head set required
Only the imagination
To evoke the feeling of the past.

He is the Great environmentalist leader
The lone knight
Protecting us from our own folly.
Please
Give him a lottery grant
To continue his quest.

clint eastwood

Probably Eastwood's oldest and most devoted Fan.

jake the rake

Mounted working urinals each descending down the side of the house

which has a portcullis entrance and a small castle moat.

High above the house stands the pulpit.

From here the sheep in the adjacent field are preached at.

The text is from an out of date Yellow Pages.

The overall effect is chaos.

This is the house that Jake built.

A wonderful monument to the eccentric mind.

john ward

```
When I think of John
Four words come to mind
Junk
Junk
Junk
Junk
He's the happy junk scientist
Many show interest in the inventions
But not the commitment.

Such is the fickle world of commerce
For this artist of inventions.
```

ed

...rocking a ten ton

alone.

Placed standing in a trance on a flat

stone.

Feeling good, going through the healing

stone.

Many attempts, many successes at water divining amongst the

stones.

Flights of fancy at the angels' runway

stone.

Wishing in Ed's fogo on the directly

stone.

A huge crystal under the bed, for good sex

stone.

All this and more at Ed's modern

Stonehenge.

tom clarkson

```
There are men out of time
Tom is a man born out of time
A non-conformist
He scares people
A strong man
With a strong belief
A strong sense of history.

The synthetic ways
Of the late Twentieth Century
Are not for him
His ways are old ways
He makes his own
Clothes
Shoes
Life.

The Green man
A true environmentalist
Without ever leaving
The council estate.
```

may fisher

```
If one needs a reason for the monarchy to continue
I can't think of a better one than to keep Royalists
                                      like May with us.

In her tea towel royal dress she adds colour
              To this sometimes drab world.
```

...waiting a in cul-de-sac on a wet winter's evening, waiting in my car

for the appointed hour to come.

Well a racing mind speeds up time.

So at the door stood a tall, pale, head shaved young man.

Lydia's Igor.

Welcomed, I entered a red, half lit living room, where I waited for Lydia to appear.

She did.

We talked and talked.

Shynesses evaporated.

I was invited to her bedroom to see and lie in a beautiful Portuguese handmade coffin.

The coffin was intended for a woman.

She had died while in Portugal;

It was saved from the cremator's fire by the husband.

Who kept it in his garage for many years.

The wife's journey was made by a different route.

Eventually the coffin came up for sale.

Lydia bought it and now the coffin is preserved,

forever.

mad mick

```
...the idea forms and some part of his body
feels the effect.
His ego gives way to the event.
He is the all giving performance artist
who invites laughter.
A lovely man
Who is always growing.
```

tom leppard

Skye has always been with me

Born in the Isle of Man

Half Scottish

Islands always attract the romantic

Those shipwrecked from life.

Skye has always been with me.

The short boat journey

The fisherman pointing

A growing figure on the small remote beach.

Stepping ashore with a gift of rum

The acceptance.

Six hours with a tattooed man

Leopard marked 98%

A refined man with a sad story.

Skye will always be with me.

lord tiverton howell

```
...entering his home, I board an open-sided elevator, that takes me up to the first floor.
Lord Tiverton is here, dressed in a white suit and a top hat.
I am greeted and asked to follow him into a large room that has, in its centre, a small ki
We stretch out on brightly coloured loungers and sip champagne... la dolce vita.
```

ron

There has to be Angels
Ron paints them
Twenty five years ago
They saved him.

From the descending devil
Angels saved Ron.

The reward for this moment of hell
Has been from that night Ron
Paints Angels
Paintings that lift up the spirit
That have a message
A warning.

My favourite
An angel
Vacuum cleaner in hand
Floating above an industrial chimney stack
Sucking up the smoke
Titled "In the Nick of Time".

captain helliwell

He rides alone.

His horse is his only companion.

To meet him is to travel in time.

He awakes every sense of the period.

You quickly realise this is no weekend game.

He rides alone.

He communes with Helliwell.

He becomes Helliwell.

I was told when we met, on that grey winter's morning.

That he would miraculously vanish, some day.

All that would be left: a pair of boots and horse shoes.

He rode off.

I sadly woke up in the late 1990s.

john slater

...having dined on carrot, garlic and sesame salad.

we set off.

From east to west coasts of Scotland.

non stop talking.

We arrive at a remote cave by the sea.

Here John spent two years removed from a more hectic life.

that brought with it several heart attacks.

Cave dwelling helped John to engage with life once more.

Life dictated by the tides.

helped him to appreciate

a

different

rhythm.

He helped me to appreciate the simpler aspects of life.

At this, the book became about the book

I simply became the messenger.

siegfried & ann

The gnome
The spirit guide
Will release you from this earth
Will help you cross over.

Ann stopped journeying westward
when Siegfried appeared.

She made an effigy
to announce his spiritual existence.

Gnomes they are fun
And beyond this many never go.

Laugh you may
There is little time left.

ed swimming pool, with large toy alligators around its edge.

crazy buffalo

When I was a boy I was a cowboy
I was John Wayne
Now I'm a man
And trying to understand
I can't be John Wayne.
If only I had the foresight to be Crazy Horse
A man of honour
A giant of a man
If only I had understood earlier
Like Crazy Buffalo
A giant of a man
Perhaps I would feel taller
Taller than I am.

It was certainly a brilliant idea of yours
to allow your subjects to write their own
assessments. Who could possibly know them-
selves or their purpose better.

jake the rake
jake the rakeke the rake

jake the rake

Jake the rake

i would like to give thanks to: Gill, Lucy, Alice, Ruth Holden, Geoff Hardy, Angela McTiernan, Ivor Cu y Woodward, Dewi Lewis, Contour Colour Ltd, and to all the people i annoyed and bothered to get this book done. i hope they think it was worth it.

photography & 'i am' text Allan Grainger   design & typography Ruth Holden   text Antony Woodward

text & illustrations
Ivor Cutler
Tom Leppard
King Arthur
May Fisher
Richard Booth
John Ward
Bodger
Ron, angel man
Lydia
Alan Fairweather
Captain Helliwell
Ed
Mad Mick
Tom Clarkson
Jake the rake
Clint Eastwood
Alan Hope
Lord Tiverton
Crazy Buffalo
John Slater
Siegfried & Ann

printed by EBS, Verona, Italy

This
above
all:
to
thine
own
self
be
true

am i am i am i am i am i am i am i am i am i am i am i am i am i am i am i am i am i am i a

Hamlet, Act 1, Scene III